# DON'T SH*T IN MY HAT AND TELL ME IT FITS BETTER

# Don't SH*T IN MY HAT AND TELL ME IT FITS BETTER

## Unedited, Un-PC, and Unapologetic

**MIKE CARACCIOLO**
**"THE KID FROM BROOKLYN"**

**with MICHAEL BENSON**

CITADEL PRESS
Kensington Publishing Corp.
www.kensingtonbooks.com

CITADEL PRESS BOOKS are published by

Kensington Publishing Corp.
850 Third Avenue
New York, NY 10022

First printing: October 2008

10  9  8  7  6  5  4  3  2  1

Printed in the United States of America

Library of Congress Control Number: 2008929363

ISBN 13: 978-0-8065-2867-0
ISBN 10: 0-8065-2867-2

To the beautiful people of Brooklyn, New York,
four million strong and each one eager and ready
to tell you to go fuck yourself!

# Contents

# Introduction: Join the Common Sense Party

Hey, the ol' Big Man is back, www.thekidfrombrooklyn.com. Some people read my first book, *Go F\*\*\* Yourself*, and they thought I was political, that I got some kind of fucking agenda. But that's horseshit.

I get e-mails all the time from people saying, "Hey, Big Man, are you a Republican or are you a Democrat? Are you on the left or are you on the right?"

I don't even know what the fuck they are talking about. Left. Right. Who the fuck knows? I never voted in my fucking life—and you wanna know why? Because as far as I'm concerned, all the politicians are fuckin' the same. They all promise you the fuckin' world, and then when they get elected, they give you fuckin' *ugatz*—nothing. Politicians are the biggest sacks of shit walking on this planet. I know homeless piss bums who got more ethics than most politicians.

Here's the guy I'd fuckin' vote for: The guy who says, "Elect me. I'm the most corrupt guy in the fuckin' world. I'm on the fuckin' take. I'm gonna make the unemployment rate go up to 15 percent. I'm gonna send five hundred fuckin' thousand more troops to Iraq. And I'm gonna rob and steal your ass blind."

That's my type of guy. Why? Because he's fuckin' honest. He comes right out and admits he's a fuckin' thief. I can respect that.

The rest of 'em give you that politician shit-eating grin, and they promise you everything in the world. They're like a fuckin' guy who wants to get laid—a stiff dick has no conscience.

Fuck the Republican Party and fuck the Democratic Party. You got those whack-job Baptist Jesus jumpers on the right and those *New York Times*-reading bleeding-heart-liberal assholes on the left. They both suck donkey dicks.

What we need is a Common Sense Party. I consider myself a common sense type guy, and if people think that makes me political, then fuck it, I'm political. The way I see it, I speak the truth—and that don't get you to the fuckin' corner in that cesspool they call politics.

For instance, take the border problem with Mexico. What a circle-jerk that's turning into. If they wanted to, they could stop this tomorrow. You put an army down there, build a wall a hundred feet high, and anybody tries to get into the country, you shoot to kill.

Or else, the minute one of them greasers crosses the Rio fuckin' Grande, you slap a uniform on him and send him straight to Iraq or Afghanistan. Watch how fast that flood of illegal aliens slows to a fuckin' trickle.

Same thing with these scumbag drug gangs we got—them Crips and Bloods and Latin Kings. Round 'em all up, ship 'em over to Baghdad, and put their beaner asses on the front lines. Gang problem solved.

But they don't want to do that. You know, the dividing line between North and South Korea is twenty feet. Twenty fuckin' feet, about the distance between me and my wife, Mona, washing the dishes in the kitchen.

On one side you've got North Koreans, on the other side

you've got South Koreans. You've got guards on either side. Anybody tries to cross from one side to the other, he gets shot. Twenty-four hours a day. Seven days a week. You think they've got an immigration problem? (Of course, they all look the same over there, but whatever.)

I'll admit it, I'm a fuckin' pessimist. I'm a "the Pepsi-glass is half-empty" type of guy. To be honest with you, I don't want to be on this Earth thirty or forty years from now. Just imagine how for-shit the world is going to be by then.

I see famine. I see this country going down like the fucking Roman Empire. The United States, if it still exists at all forty years from now, is going to be a second-rate country. It ain't gonna be the biggest power in the world anymore. You can't stay on top forever. Nobody can.

There ain't gonna be enough land to grow the food to feed the population. And there are too many people. Look at the pollution in the air. There are too many cars. There's too much everything. How are you going to feed people if the population of the United States goes to, say, six hundred million, and China goes to ten billion?

And I've had this vision now for at least ten years. I see turmoil. It'll be the rich or the poor. It'll be like in ancient times. The kings and the queens and the peasants. No more middle class. The middle class will be totally wiped off the face of the Earth. You can see it now. If you can't see it, you're blind.

The solution is a tough thing to call, but you gotta control the birth rate. You gotta limit every family to one child. There's just so much land on this planet. It's gonna be all filled with houses and there'll be no more farms. How are you going to grow the food to feed these people? Everything's going to be made synthetically, in factories. That's where food is going to come from. And only the rich, only the people that can afford it, will be able to eat naturally grown vegetables, meat, fish. It's common sense. The population keeps getting bigger and bigger. How are you going to feed people? Can you imagine fifty years from now, if it keeps up this pace?

It might be too fuckin' late to fix New York. If anybody had any foresight, they would have made the bridges and the roads a fuckload larger than they are. You only can squeeze a certain amount of cars onto the road and roadways are too small. If I could change anything right now, I wouldn't allow private cars. I'd build large parking lots and people would have to come into the city by tram or by subway train.

Another prediction I've got is that they'll build in outer space. They'll build another country up there. They'll take a rocket ship to the moon or any planet, and it'll be like taking a plane to California. That's the only way they can do it.

What about water? When I was a kid in Brooklyn, if you told me I had to pay twenty-five cents for a bottle of water, I'd have laughed at you. Look at the water in the street today. Fifty different kinds of bottled water. People take water for granted. Water is the number one commodity in the world. Forget about gold, platinum, plutonium. What do you do if you run out of water? You're going to have to limit the amount of water people use to take a shower or bath. The amount of water consumption every day is enormous. People don't think of these things. I think of it. Do you know how much water is consumed in a twenty-four-hour period, how many billions of gallons? Where is this water going to come from, fifty years from now? Water will be worth gold. Take it from the Big Man. There are too many fuckin' people on this planet and there ain't enough water to support all of them. The problem is only going to get bigger and bigger.

Pretty soon we'll be just like the fuckin' Arabs with their fuckin' oil—only the water will be worth more than the oil. Ten years from now, water will be worth more than oil. They'll be gettin' sixty fuckin' dollars a barrel for fresh water.

So people, youse who live here in the Big fuckin' Apple and

youse who come here to visit and wave like fuckin' lunatics in the background during the fuckin' *Today Show*, take advantage of New York while you still can, before it goes completely down the toilet.

Go for a walk. You can't go in Manhattan and breathe fresh air, because there's no such thing as fresh air in Manhattan. You just can't breathe anymore with all the high-rises and the air-conditioning units blowing out, all the people smoking. Manhattan is a small island. It's not made for breathing.

Anyway, I may not be fuckin' political but I am the fuckin' voice of the people. I been getting two, three hundred phone calls a day these days. I get calls from Los Angeles, Las Vegas, Nevada, Pittsburgh, Rochester, New York, Miami, Florida, all across the fuckin' country, east to west, north to south.

They all say the same thing. They want to thank the Big Man for tellin' it like it is, for puttin' some truth into their lives. The world is filled with so many fuckin' lies these days that all you got to do is tell the truth, to look at things and describe the way they really are, and people feel grateful.

Now, the Big Man ain't getting' rich off this, the computer stuff, the stand-up comedy, the book deals. None of it is fuckin' making me rich. I'm payin' my bills but that's about it. But let me make a promise to you, dear readers, if the Big Man ever does get to be rich and famous because of the things I say, because of telling the truth in a world full of fuckin' lies, I'm gonna spread that money around.

Oh yeah, I'm gonna spread that money around like butter on a fuckin' piece of bread.

# Acknowledgments

The Big Man wants to thank the following people for their help in the creation of this book: editor of the people Gary Goldstein; agent with a heart o' fuckin' gold Jake Elwell, my partner in crime Kevin Helmick, and especially to my wife, Mona, who still gets the job done if you know what I'm fuckin' talkin' about. And thanks to all youse who put the ol' Big Man on the fuckin' map. You know who you are.

> *If they wanted to, they could stop the fuckin' immigration problem tomorrow. You put an army down there, build a wall a hundred feet high, and anybody tries to get into the country, you shoot to kill.*

# Let Me Tell You Something, Fellas: Stay Single

My son's friend is getting married. He met this woman on the fuckin' computer, on one of them fuckin' online dating services. You got to be out of your fuckin' mind to go on a computer today and look for a fuckin' woman.

There are thousands of fuckin' women with fuckin' personal ads on the computer. Hey, Mr. Fuckin' Bachelor, do you think those women give a fuck about you? Do you think they're lookin' for fuckin' love? Fuck, no. They are after one fuckin' thing: cash.

Let me tell you something, fellas. Take it from someone who fuckin' knows. Once you get married to a woman, ain't nothin' you do ever good enough. If you get 'em a house, they want a bigger house. If you get 'em a Mercedes-Benz, they want a fuckin' Rolls-Royce. If you get 'em a fuckin' Rolls-Royce, they want a fuckin' jet airplane.

It don't make no difference what you do for a fuckin' woman, it ain't good enough. If you make a million dollars a year, they want you to make two fuckin' million dollars a year. If you screw 'em twice a night, they want to be screwed five times a night. (As the great Mick Jagger once said, "I ain't got that much fuckin' jam!")

If you take 'em to the best fuckin' restaurant and you buy 'em the best fuckin' food, it ain't good enough. So let me tell ya, any fuckin' young guys out there who are thinkin' o' gettin' married, go get your fuckin' head examined. You got to be out of your fuckin' mind. You can't please any fuckin' woman.

1

So take it from the voice of the fuckin' people: Stay single, you stupid bastards!

*If you get 'em a Mercedes-Benz, they want a fuckin' Rolls-Royce. If you get 'em a fuckin' Rolls-Royce, they want a fuckin' jet airplane.*

## Retard Suicide Bombers

So just when you think the Muslim terrorist assholes can't sink any fuckin' lower, what the fuck do they do? They strap suicide belts onto a couple of retards who don't know any better, send 'em into a market, and then detonate the bombs by remote control! Killed over a hundred people. I mean, these fuckin' Muslim terrorists are scum—they ain't even got the fuckin' balls to do the deed themselves—now they're grabbin' retards off the fuckin' street to do their fuckin' dirty work!

This is what we're dealing with now.

What worries the Big Man is, we got plenty of retards right here in America them terrorist cocksuckers could use to do the same thing here—in a mall or a Wal-Mart or a fuckin' supermarket.

I mean, shit, you go into one of them Stop & Shops we got around here and there's always a bunch of them retards bagging groceries.

Who's gonna suspect a retard of being a suicide bomber? Some of these retards can't even stop drooling long enough to bag up a sack of fuckin' toilet paper.

How hard would it be for some Muslim bastard to say, "Hey, kid, if you wear this belt under your shirt, I'll give you a Hershey bar."

What's the kid gonna say, no thanks? He don't know any better 'cause he's a retard. Do the fuckin' math!

Fuck, no. Five minutes later, you're gonna see a fuckin' mushroom cloud over the goddamn strip mall.

They did in Baghdad, they'll do it here, mark my words.

These are the kinds of lowlife, murdering cocksucking savages who are slipping into America by the hundreds every fuckin' day.

So next time you're in a supermarket or a shopping center or wherever, and you see someone offering a retard a Hershey bar, get the fuck out of there pronto.

Anyway, think about it.


# Waitin' for Osama

The Big Man was watchin' Fox News the other day and saw that they're waiting for a new fuckin' video from Osama bin Laden. They got the word that he made a new video. What? What the fuck? Who got the word that he made a new fuckin' video? I mean, come on, give me a fuckin' break.

You want to tell me that, with all of the fuckin' money they're offering for that terrorist motherfucker's head, ain't no one gonna rat the cocksucker out? They just gonna call up Fox News and say he made a new video so Fox should be expecting it? Bull-fucking-shit. They're offering fifty fuckin' million dollars for the head of Osama bin Laden on a fuckin' platter and still ain't no one coming forward. What the fuck is up with that?

And all the technology we fuckin' got today and we can't find this guy? I mean, we send guys to the fuckin' moon! And we can't find one fuckin' Muslim terrorist? I can't fuckin' believe it.

Me, I'm a sensible guy. I say, we outsource the fuckin' search for Osama bin Laden. I say, we contract the job out to the Chinese. I mean, we give the Chinese everything else, why not the job of putting the hit on Bin Fuckin' Laden?

The Chinese make all of our fuckin' clothes, all of our kids' fuckin' toys, all of our computer parts. They make everything! Give the fuckin' Chinese the contract to find this fuckin' Osama bin Laden and don't you worry. Take it from the Big Man, they'll find that son of a fuckin' bitch. They'll send a two-fuckin'-million-man army.

You don't fuck around with them fuckin' Chinese. They'll go into Afghanistan, they'll cover Iraq, they'll be all over the whole fuckin' Middle East, and they'll find the rat bastard. They'll put some ass-wipe terrorist up against a fuckin' wall, put a fuckin' meat cleaver to his head, and say, "You tell us where fuckin' Osama bin Laden is or you won't be shoppin' at the fuckin' Big and Tall store anymore. Tell us where he is or you won't have to worry about combing your hair anymore, on account o' your fuckin' body is gonna stop at your fuckin' neck!"

The Chinese would find him. Oh yeah, they'd find him and, when they do, they're gonna turn him into a fuckin' dish: Osama bin Laden Egg Foo Fuckin' Yung! With a side of Osama Chop Fuckin' Suey!

*They're offering fifty fuckin' million dollars for the head of Osama bin Laden on a fuckin' platter and still ain't no one coming forward. What the fuck is up with that?*

# Why You Can't Get Miller in a Bodega No More

You know what a fuckin' bodega is? For those of you who don't come from New York City, let the Big Man explain. Throughout New York—in Brooklyn, the Bronx, Staten Island, and Queens—there are thousands, maybe fuckin' millions, of fuckin' bodegas. A bodega is a Hispanic-owned grocery store. They're usually on the corner and they're open twenty-four hours a day. They sell soda, beer, cigarettes, candy, Lotto tickets, reefer, and crack cocaine. Twenty-four fuckin' hours a day.

Well, the Big Man has just learned that the fuckin' Miller High Life company, makers of Miller High Life Beer, have decided to stop selling their beer in all the bodegas of New York. Those people who owned those fuckin' bodegas had the balls to charge twenty dollars—twenty fuckin' dollars!—for a two-dollar crack pipe. Can you imagine that? Now the greedy bastards are going to pay the ultimate price. Now they can't sell Miller High Life no more. I don't know why.

# Tie a Yellow Ribbon Around Your Fat Ass, Tony Orlando

So I was talking with my old pal from Bensonhurst, Willie Potatoes.

Willie tells me he went for a checkup and his doctor said he needs to lose fifty pounds.

The Big Man is here to tell you, at our age, Willie's doc might as well have told him to lose five hundred fuckin' pounds. Losing weight ain't so easy when you're over fifty.

So's Willie's watching TV and he sees this commercial

where Tony Orlando's hawking some shit called Nutri-System, where they send you food, you eat it, and you lose weight.

They show a picture of this Tony Orlando when he weighed, like, five hundred pounds and looked like a fuckin' beached whale. I seen that commercial myself.

Thing is, even after Tony Orlando says he lost all this weight, and went from wearing fuckin' pants the size of a fuckin' circus tent down to a size 34, he still looks like a fat schlub.

Whatever. Willie is all excited. He says, "Seems like a good deal. They send you steak and lasagna and all kinds of great shit. They even give you fuckin' desserts!"

Now, I got to explain that Willie Potatoes didn't get that name for no reason. The man loves to eat. The guy could even put me to shame when it comes to stuffing your face. I once seen him put away an entire two-pound standing rib roast—and that was as an appetizer.

I mean the guy eats like he had three assholes.

So he orders the 144-item meal package, but not from their 800 number. The cheap shit actually goes to eBay and gets it for half of what the Nutri-System people would've charged.

I mean, who the fuck buys breakfast, lunch, and dinner on fuckin' eBay? Willie Potatoes, that's who.

A few days later, the UPS guy delivers the goods. Willie's beside himself—there's scrambled eggs and peanut butter pastries and fettuccine Alfredo and cheese tortellini and pot roast and pizza, the whole ball of wax, ninety meals and fifty desserts, supposed to last you a month at least.

Long story short, Willie tries one meal but it don't fill him up. So he has another. And another after that. He polishes off the whole month's worth in two fuckin' days and he's still hungry. So he goes down to McDonalds and eats ten Happy Meals.

Instead of losing weight with that Nutri-System, Willie gains twenty fuckin' pounds. That's some fuckin' diet.

Willie said, "If I ever run into that greasy bastard Tony Orlando, I'm gonna kick his fat ass all the way to Cleveland."

The moral is, when something sounds too fuckin' good to be true, it usually is.

Anyway, think about it.

## Columbia Uni-fuckin'-versity

You know, about a year ago, the Big Man, being the Voice, the Voice of the People, wanted to reach out. The Big Man wanted to give back. That's what I'm all about. So I offered my services to fuckin' Columbia University, the fuckin' Ivy League school up there at the top of Manhattan.

Now the school is jam-packed with book-smart people. They gotcher bona fide horn-rim glasses geniuses up there, but what the fuck do these people know about life? Doodely-fuckin' squat, that's what the fuck they know.

So the Big Man decided to volunteer his services, to address a gathering of Columbia University students and faculty on the subject of street smarts. Nothin' fancy—just the fundamentals of street smarts. Don't make eye contact with crazy people. Shit like that.

So I called up the lady who sets up the public speaking engagements at Columbia University.

I said, "Hello, Mrs. Bird. My name is Mike Caracciolo. I have a Web site on the Internet—www.thekidfrombrooklyn.com. I want to go up there and offer you my services, give your students and faculty a little piece of education that they ain't gettin' in the classroom."

She said, "Mr. Caracciolo, we will have to examine your Web site, and we'll get back to you in a couple of days."

Three days later, Mrs. Bird called me back.

"Mr. Caracciolo, I am very sorry to inform you, but due to your coarseness and your profane use of the English language, Columbia University, one of the most prestigious schools in the United States, cannot accept your offer to speak to our students and faculty. Columbia University only accepts men and women of honor to speak at our podium."

You know, I felt kind of bad at first that they wouldn't let me go up there and speak to these kids about what I know about street smarts. Then, then! I learned that this fuckin' Momo Onmydinnerjacket, the fuckin' dictator of Iran, this fuckin' terrorist, was going to speak at Columbia University. They wouldn't let me speak because they did not consider me a man of honor but they were going to allow this terrorist motherfucker a place behind their sacred fuckin' podium. This fuckin' university has the balls to call itself prestigious when it makes fuckin' decisions like that?

He's okay but I'm not. Here's a guy who starves fuckin' 60 percent of his people. He supplies a safe haven for all of the fuckin' terrorists. He sends millions of fuckin' dollars to Hezbollah. He makes fuckin' weapons to kill our soldiers. And his sole purpose in creating nuclear weapons is to annihilate the fuckin' state of Israel.

Now the fuckin' truth comes out. Now we fuckin' know what Columbia University is all about. So here's a tip to all you fuckin' parents out there who pay boocoo fuckin' bucks

*This fuckin' university has the balls to call itself prestigious when it makes fuckin' decisions like that?*

to send your fuckin' kids to Columbia University, and here's a tip to all the people who donate their hard-earned money to all of the corporations that donate millions of dollars to this prestigious school: get your fuckin' head examined!

See where your fuckin' money is going?

## Leave Britney Alone!

Hey, remember back when Britney fuckin' Spears was going to make her big comeback, and she appeared on the MTV Awards? It was all over the fuckin' news. Every fuckin' person and his mother started taking a steamy dump on fuckin' Britney.

They said she put on a lousy performance. They said she was over-fuckin'-weight. Let me tell you something about the way Britney looked. Seventy-five percent of the fuckin' women in the fuckin' world would cut off a finger or a toe to look like Britney Spears looked that night.

They would fuckin' pay to have a body like Britney. I mean, come on, give me a fuckin' break. She's got two fuckin' children! She gave birth to two fuckin' children! After that, you can only do so fuckin' much. What do they expect? Do they want her to go on the fuckin' MTV Awards lookin' like fuckin' Twiggy or something, a razor-thin waif who looks like she's living on V8 and tree bark? No fuckin' way.

Me, personally, I think Britney has still got it fuckin' goin' on. She has got some great fuckin' body. And the Big Man thinks she put on a great performance that night. I couldn't fuckin' take my eyes off her.

For a person who was under the fuckin' influence, she did a fuckin' great job out there. I mean, she was liquored up and doped up and, taking that into fuckin' consideration, she did a hell of a job!

Imagine me and you getting up on the fuckin' stage all

liquored up and doped up and trying to put on a fuckin' show. Puh-fuckin'-leaze! Leave Britney alone. Give her a fuckin' break. She's trying her fuckin' best!

All kidding aside, did you see that clip on YouTube of that guy with the eye makeup who got all weepy about the press's hounding Britney Spears? Of course, if the press really wanted to bug Britney they would leave her alone.

Five minutes without any fuckin' attention and she'd be shaving her fuckin' head again. But back to the clip, I think they should use that "leave Britney alone" kid as an example. They should give that YouTube clip to all of the teachers in America.

They should play the clip for their classes and then say, "See kids, see what happens when you take fuckin' drugs."

*I think Britney has still got it fuckin' goin' on.*

## Get Me to Gitmo

This here government of the United States of America has got the wrong fuckin' idea. Put me in charge of these fuckin' prisoners, these fuckin' detainees, down there in fuckin' Guantanamo Bay in Cuba. Detainees. That's what they call terrorist motherfuckers these days.

I'd have a fuckin' tailor come in, measure 'em all. They'd all get $3,000 suits. They'd get beautiful shirts. Beautiful shoes. I'd put 'em all in a king-size bed and give 'em all high-definition TVs the size of a fuckin' movie screen.

Then I'd feed 'em the best food money can buy: Peter Luger steaks, the best wines and liquors. And after all that, I'd send 'em in with the world's most gorgeous women. The most gorgeous women naked. And I'd let these prisoners do whatever they want with these women.

Pretty soon the word would get out that this is the greatest fuckin' jail in the whole fuckin' world, and all of those other terrorist motherfuckers out there will be throwing up their hands. They'll say, "I surrender. I fuckin' surrender. Take me to fuckin' Guantanamo Bay." They'll be beggin' to get caught, beggin' to go to that fuckin' jail. They'll say, "Allah sent me here. Praise be to Allah."

I'm just jokin'. Here's how I really feel. I don't want to tell you how many e-mails I've gotten from numskull knuckleheads with shit for brains out there in fuckin' World Wide Web land saying that 9/11 was a hoax and that the United States actually attacked ourselves so that we would have a reason to go to war. I guess there are always going to be loony kazoos who think this way. There are people who think we bombed our own ships at Pearl Harbor so we'd have a fuckin' excuse to go to war with the Japs.

I watched the O'Reilly Factor. They had a woman on there complainin' about the way we treat the prisoners at Guantanamo Bay. She said that water-boardin' and the like was fuckin' cruel and unusual punishment. We coerce them, she said.

She complained that we were always playing loud music when they were trying to get their beauty sleep. Boo-hoo, she said; a prisoner at Gitmo is trying to catch some z's and the Red Hot Fuckin' Chili Peppers are comin' out of the fuckin' boom box.

She was complainin' that we keep the cells too cold and was pleading for more humane treatment for these scumbags, these terrorists, who conspired to take down the World Trade Center. Let me tell you something, lady:

Them fuckin' terrorists had better pray that I'm never in fuckin' charge of that fuckin' jail down there in fuckin' Cuba. I would start with one finger at a time. Chopping. Then another finger, two, and another finger, three, and if they don't fuckin' talk I move to the toes, eleven, twelve, thirteen. And take my word for it, them terrorist motherfuckers better hope I don't have to count to twenty-one.

I'd get the information out of them. I'd have a fuckin' doctor there to make sure they don't fuckin' bleed to death. This lady who wants humane treatment for these prisoners doesn't understand something. She doesn't understand a key fact: THESE ARE FUCKIN' TERRORISTS! What are you, fuckin' insane? These are fuckin' murderers.

Think about those poor people who got up early in the morning one day and went to work in the World Trade Center and never made it back home. Think about them, lady. They got fuckin' killed for fuckin' nothin'.

The prisoners down there in Cuba are terrorists. Are you fuckin' insane, lady? They are terrorists. So anytime anybody says anything about what they do to these fuckin' prisoners, I got one fuckin' thing to say to you: Go fuck yourself! Read my lips. Go fuck yourself!

*Boo-hoo, she said; a prisoner at Gitmo is trying to catch some z's and the Red Hot Fuckin' Chili Peppers are comin' out of the fuckin' boom box.*

# Whiny Americans

We got more choices in this country than any other country in the fuckin' universe and people are still complaining. Let me tell you what I mean. Last winter, the newsmen on the fuckin' TV were calling for a blizzard for fuckin' days and, sure enough, ever since they got these fuckin' satellites and computers and such shit, these guys know what the fuck they are talking about, most of the time. Sometimes.

This time they called it right and, just when they said it would, the fuckin' snow started comin' down. Now, I know I waited to the last second but I said to Mona, "Mona, I better get to the fuckin' store and get us some fuckin' supplies just in case we get fuckin' snowed in."

I got to the fuckin' A&P and the place was packed. Everybody was fuckin' griping: They only got the smooth fuckin' peanut butter. They ain't got the chunky. They only got the tuna fish packed in water. They ain't got the tuna fish packed in fuckin' oil. Pack this in fuckin' oil, lady!

I couldn't even get a fuckin' grocery cart. But you know what? There was still plenty of food on the shelves. So I stopped to think about just how lucky we have it here in the U.S. of A.

Boy, the choices we got. The fruits. The vegetables. There were thousands of different types of products in that fuckin' store. Imagine if an American had to go live in Russia or China. Imagine the grocery stores they got over there. They probably got shit on a fuckin' shingle. It would be nothin' compared to what we got here.

The American people are all spoiled. Imagine the whining Americans would do if they were in a grocery store in fuckin' China, "Oooooh, Harry. They don't have this. They don't have that. What will we do? Ohhhhh, what the fuck will we doooooo?"

So next time you're in the fuckin' supermarket and you're whining your ass off about something, the line at the cash register is moving too fuckin' slow for your liking or some- thing, I say, shut the fuck up, you douche bag, and move the fuck to China.

You should be fuckin' grateful that you eat every fuckin' day. You go to fuckin' China and you wake up in the mornin' with a fuckin' rice paddy up your ass. You end up losing eighty pounds in fuckin' three months.

So get the fuck out of here with your whining bullshit in the fuckin' grocery store. This is the United States of fuckin' America, the best fuckin' country in the whole fuckin' uni- verse. That's right. You read that right. It ain't just the best fuckin' country on Earth. It's the best fuckin' country on fuckin' Mars and Jupiter!

> *This is the United States of fuckin' America, the best fuckin' country in the whole fuckin' universe.*

## Airport Rest Rooms

Now, I know you heard that story about Republican senator Larry Craig out of Idaho. For about three days, that was all the fuck you heard about. They said he was trying to solicit homosexual sex in an airport toilet.. He did this by touching his foot to the foot of the guy in the next stall. Well, here is a word in Senator Craig's defense:

When was the last time you people were in an airport rest room? Do you see the size of those fuckin' stalls? You couldn't fit a midget in there. Puttin' the Big Man in one of those rest rooms is like trying to squeeze Rosie O'Donnell into Scarlet Johansen's fuckin' panties. I can't even fit my fuckin' ass in there. I'm six foot six, four hundred fuckin' pounds.

I got to grease myself down with Vaseline to fit into one of them stalls. And once I set my ass on the bowl and do my business, there's no fuckin' room to wipe my ass.

So this Larry Craig touched a guy's foot with his foot and they arrested him.

If I touch a guy's foot with my foot it ain't because I'm lookin' to get a blow job—it's because I'm tryin' to get my fuckin' shit to go in the fuckin' bowl instead of on the fuckin' floor or down my fuckin' leg.

Bottom line: Make them public rest rooms larger so big people like me can fit in them!

As for that Larry Craig, I don't think it was an accident. He's thin, so he must have been cruising for some action, the hypocritical fudge-packer.

*You got to cover me in fuckin' lard and get ten guys to push just to get me in the fuckin' stall. There's no room to wipe your fuckin' ass in there.*

## A Lot of Fuckin' Shit Has Happened to Me Since My First Book

A lot of fuckin' shit has happened to me since my first book, *Go F\*\*\* Yourself*. I went from being a regular guy who wanted to tell people about the shit that pissed me off to whatcha might call a celebrity.

My stand-up career is thriving. I been workin' out there in Vegas and in Manhattan at the Gotham Comedy Club where all the fuckin' big stars go. Been packin' places. And I'm drawing the right kind of crowds, too. The Big Man's type of crowds, good people who understand my fuckin' humor.

Everybody fuckin' knows who I am now. I walk down the street and folks say, "Hey, Big Man, give 'em hell." It's like I'm Harry fuckin' Truman or something. They did a special on the cable network VH1, counting down the biggest celebrities on the Internet, and I was one of their featured acts.

They called me "one of the Internet's most prolific pundits." That means I got a lot of fuckin' opinions, but you already knew that. They had some joker on there doing an imitation of me and I could tell he thought I was fuckin' drunk. It's like he didn't get it. I couldn't be more sober. Fuck. If I was drunk, I wouldn't be so fuckin' pissed off.

They had me making comments about other Internet celebrities and other Internet celebrities commenting on me. You know LonelyGirl? She said I cussed more than any other human being alive. Shows what she fuckin' knows. She's plenty fuckin' cute but I'll bet she's never been on Flatbush Avenue in her life. If she had, she'd know I talk like a fuckin' Sunday school teacher compared to some of the fucks they got in Brooklyn.

I say things that other people ain't got the guts to say. That's what I do. The swearing just comes naturally on account of I'm genuinely pissed off. It ain't an act. You think

I'm pretending to think Starbucks is too expensive? You got to be out of your fuckin' mind.

I always thought I'd be famous but I thought it would be on account of I'm a great actor. This Internet shit came as a complete surprise to me. It started in 2004 when I was rantin' and ravin' about some shit that pissed me off, I don't remember what the fuck it was, and a co-worker told me I should put it on the Internet.

I said, what the fuck.

So this guy hooked up a webcam and he said, "You talk into here, say what you want to say, make it under three minutes, and I'll put it on the Internet."

Now it's three fuckin' years later and I am known around the world. Not just in Brooklyn, not just in New Jersey, but all the way around the fuckin' world.

The rants led to a weekly call-in show on the Web, and after that I got gigs doing stand-up comedy. That's a lot of fun. A lot of comics, they dread being heckled. I'm just the fuckin' opposite. Somebody tried to heckle me, I got a big mouth and I got no trouble shouting him down. All I got to do is tell him to go fuck himself, and the crowd is fuckin' on my side.

My latest gig is I'm the host of an Internet show called Viral Vidiocy. *Vidiocy* being a cross between "video" and "idiot." That's what I do: I fuckin' interview the idiots who put videos on the Internet that demonstrate precisely the manner in which they are fuckin' idiots. It's sort of like a cross between YouTube and *Jackass*.

I didn't like the gig because you spend your time talkin' to fuckin' idiots. On the other hand, you usually come off looking pretty goddamn smart, you know, by comparison. The thing is really edited slick so while I'm interviewing these creative morons, you get to see the idiotic stuff they do.

In the first episode, I interviewed a guy named Chris from

Austin, Texas. His claim to fuckin' fame was that he shot a bottle rocket off in his ass.

I started off by asking him, "Hey, Chris, how's that fucking ass of yours?"

Chris said to me, "Uhhhhhh, I got burned—but it's fine now."

"How did you come up with the idea of sticking a bottle rocket up your ass, Chris?"

"Well, we were all out there, just the neighborhood kids. My brother Ryan had the idea. He said someone should shoot a bottle rocket off in their ass, and he wasn't going to do it."

I said, "I did some crazy shit when I was a kid, Chris, but I never got anywhere near to shooting a bottle rocket off in my ass."

Now we're looking at the video of this. Chris has got his drawers down and his fuckin' legs up in the air. He looks like a fuckin' nymphomaniac at a gang bang with his fuckin' legs up in the air like that. And the others are having an argument. Nobody wants to be the one to hold Chris's legs back. No one wants to be the one to light the bottle rocket. That shows you right there the difference between cowardice and bravery. (As well as the difference between intelligence and stupidity.) Here's one guy who's willing to have a fucking bottle rocket go off in his ass and the others ain't got the fuckin' nads to light the fuse! Finally Chris's brother torches the sucker and off it goes in Chris's ass.

Chris said, "I could see the sparks going off and it burned me. I kept my ass clenched the whole time. I couldn't unclench it because it just kept burning me."

"Did your balls get burned, too?" I asked.

"No, I held those. I kept a hand on them the whole time."

"You're fuckin' out of your mind, you know that?" I said. "Are you fuckin' insane? Let me speak to your mother."

And so Chris's mother comes on the line. She's sitting there on a couch with Chris and Chris's brother, the idea man.

"How does this make you feel as a mother, Kelly?" I asked.

"I'm real proud of Chris for this," she said—and I think she was fuckin' serious. "If he wants to stick fire in his ass, then that's what he wants to do."

You got to admire a woman who is willing to support her son in all of his endeavors, no matter how fucking out of his mind he might be. Then I learned that the mom was the one who was working the camcorder when the bottle rocket went off up Chris's ass.

"What were you thinking?" I asked her.

It was Chris who answered. He said, "We weren't thinking of the consequences of getting burned. In case anybody is wondering, I don't recommend the smell of burnt ass hair. It doesn't smell all that great."

In the next episode of the show, we took our viewers all the way to fuckin' New Zealand, to talk to Graham, Nathan, and Matt. These were the guys who made the "Kid vs. Car" video. As you fuckin' might imagine, the fuckin' car won. Graham drove it, Nathan got hit, and Matt filmed it. We showed the video. Now this car did not give Nathan a fucking love tap. It was moving pretty good. It hit Nathan so hard that he flipped up over the hood of the car, over the roof, and came down hard in the middle of the street.

"Hey, Nathan," I said. "I got to tell you, you got to be the dumbest motherfucker on the planet, steppin' in front of a fuckin' car like that. Why? Why did you do it, Nathan?"

"I had a friend who jumped off a really tall building," he said. "So I got hit by a car to show I was as brave as him."

"Are you a professional? I mean, you could have gotten killed," I said.

"No, no, we practiced a lot. I got hurt a few times before we got it right," he said. In other words, he did it for fuckin' free. He did it repeatedly for fuckin' free.

"I wouldn't do that for all the money in the fuckin' world,"

**This is Mr. Fleeger, who owned Fleeger's Hardware on E. 98th Street. The rumor around Canarsie was, if he caught you shoplifting, he'd take you into the back and put your tongue in a vice. (author's collection)**

I said. "For all my luck, I'd get fuckin' killed. How did this come off? How did you think of it?"

"We used to do it to freak out little kids," Nathan said. The show's editors at this point inserted the sound of crickets to show the emptiness of Nathan's brain.

"Let me ask you something. What would you have done

if something went wrong? Graham, don't you realize that you could have fuckin' killed him?"

Graham just laughed, a long insane laugh like a fuckin' mad scientist who was plotting to rule the fucking world.

"Didn't your mothers ever teach you not to play in the fuckin' street?" I asked. 'That's got to be the dumbest fucking thing I've ever seen in my fucking life."

"We were just bored and we had nothing to do," Graham said, finally pulling himself out of his laughing jag.

"What were you guys smoking? A fucking crack pipe?" I asked. "What about the car?"

"It was actually another guy's car. The windshield broke and I got glass all over me," Nathan said.

"Hey, over there in New Zealand, did anyone ever tell you to go fuck yourselves?"

"Not really," they all said.

"Well, that's the way we talk back here in Brooklyn," I explained. "When we come across people who do stupid things we say, 'Hey stupid, go fuck yourself!'"

Then, finally, at last, I found a fucking molecule of intelligence in these wackos. I asked them if they would do it again and they said, "Definitely not." Which only goes to show, everyone learns at his own fucking pace.

In the next episode, I talked with Zack, Paul, and Cody from down there in fuckin' Tennessee.

"Now I can't even fuckin' turn on the Internet without seeing someone putting Mentos in a soda bottle. You get a fuckin' Old Faithful geyser of soda shooting up into the fucking air. But you guys tried it a little different, right?"

"Yeah, we did it and then we put the bottle cap back on the bottle," Zack said. "Then we turned it upside down and took the cap off." In other words, they made a fuckin' rocket.

"What kind of a dipshit do you have to be to throw candy into a bottle of pop? Back where I come from, that's considered a waste of both candy and pop. What's the matter with you guys? Ain't you got no women down there you could fool around with?"

They just laughed, which I took as a no.

"What sort of response have you gotten from puttin' this shit on the Internet? Are you guys famous?"

"When we first did the soda rocket, we thought it was pretty cool and we thought some people might like it, so we put it on the Internet." It was a pretty good answer—to a completely different fucking question. I guess they ain't too famous.

"You know, when I first heard about this shit I thought, come on! There's got to be better things to do than put fucking breath mints in a bottle of soda pop. I heard you guys are going into the parking lot now to show us a trick. Go ahead, I'm dying to see it."

And so they blasted off a soda rocket. You remember putting a cherry bomb under an empty soup can? You could get that thing to go sixty, seventy feet in the air. This was a lot like that.

"Well, guys, I feel a lot dumber for having talked with yiz," I said.

The next episode was one of my favorites. I interviewed a diminutive black fella named Shawn who came from Mobile, Alabama, and talked a little bit like Buckwheat. I introduced the show this way, "Shawn is part of a worldwide phenomenon that is taking place in his tiny neighborhood. Everybody thinks they saw a fucking leprechaun. It was even on the news."

They showed a news report of a bunch of people all mingling alongside a street with shit-eating grins on their faces. The announcer said, "Curiosity leads to large crowds in a Mobile community and everyone uses binoculars, camcorders, and even phone cameras to take pictures."

Then they showed this guy with about three teeth in his mouth who said, "It depinably look like a lepachaun to me."

He sounded a little bit like Buckwheat, too. Apparently, there's a fucking neighborhood in Mobile where everyone sounds like Buckwheat.

"I think it's just something casting a shadow," a critic opined. "Maybe comin' from another limb or something."

Then I said, "This is a world exclusive. What are you gonna tell the people, Shawn?"

The little guy grinned. "That's me that was in the tree," he said. "I was in the tree just chillin' and folks was throwing rocks and stuff at me. That's me in the tree, on account of I am a real fucking leprychaun. Hi-dee-ho. A . . . real . . . fuckin'. . . leprychaun. Any questions you want to ask me?"

"I might believe this shit if you lived in Ireland," I said. "For Chrissakes. Alabama? Come on! Give me a fuckin' break."

"Leprychauns trabel. They try to catch me for my gold, but they cannot catch the leprychaun."

"You got a lot of people out there who actually believe this is true, and it's circling the world on the Internet. Now there's a woman on the news report who accuses the leprechaun of being a crackhead. Shawn, you're not into drugs and climbing into trees, are ya?"

"Leprychauns don't take no crack," Shawn said. "We get drunk and we get high but, other than that, we don't smoke no crack."

"You're doin' a pretty good job down there, Shawn. You have started a big phenomenon, and you got 'em all fooled. Am I right or not right?"

"I ain't foolin' nobody, Big Man. I am a real fuckin' leprychaun."

"Hey, Shawn?"

"Yeah."

"There's a lot of women out there who want to know if a leprechaun is magically delicious. Are you magically delicious?"

"Yes. I'm madically delisis. All the womens wants me. But they cannot catch me. That's the problem."

"If you really are a leprechaun, good luck to ya," I said. "God bless ya!" After all, the little guy seemed kind of sincere.

"Thank you, Big Man," Shawn said, signing off. "Hi-dee-ho!"

The following week I interviewed a "vidiot" from Middletown, Connecticut. His name was Reh-Dogg. I asked him how he was doin'. Reh-Dogg had a music video on the Internet, singing a song called "Why Must I Cry?" Thing was, Reh-Dogg couldn't hit a note with a fucking sniper rifle. Every fucking note he sang was flat. I mean fl-a-a-a-t. Flatter than a fuckin' ninety-year-old Asian woman. The thing that made Reh-Dogg popular was that his singing voice might've been bogus, but his emotions were fuckin' real. He would sing his fuckin' song, which sounded like a vocally challenged dog howling at the fucking moon, but real fucking tears would be streaming down his cheeks. The only thing uglier than his voice was his face.

"The Big Man would be the first to admit that he's not too easy on the eyes," I said to Reh-Dogg, "but you are one ugly son of a bitch! This scene of you singing in the shower, it looks like a porn movie to me."

"It's not porn. I was just trying something different and I came up with that," he said. "I got a lot of attention."

"Your skin looks kinda smooth down there. What the fuck are you using? Nair?"

"Nothin'. I'm juss naturally smooth, I guess. It's a God-gibben giff."

"A God-given gift, well, God bless ya. Hey Reh-Dogg, the whole world wants to know: What makes you cry?"

"Many things, but currently my ex-girlfriend. She's crazy and she just up and left, so that's makin' me cry. People stealin' from me, that's makin' me cry, too."

"You're in bad shape, Reh-Dogg. Why did your girlfriend leave you?"

"She's crazy."

"Sorry to hear that—makin' a poor guy like you cry like

that. That scene of you on your video where you're up in the woods was pretty good. Did you have a professional director shoot your video?"

"No, I was just up in the woods in the Avon Mountains just runnin' around havin' my buddy film it and it came out pretty good."

"What kind of a reaction have you gotten to your video, Reh-Dogg?"

"At first all of the reactions came from haters, from people telling me that I suck, that I should quit. But lately I been getting feedback from the West Coast and from down south and they been showing me lots of love."

"I don't know what the fuck that means, but whatever it means I want to wish you the best of luck," I said.

The next week, I talked to a guy in Norway who made weird oral noises and then edited them so that he sounded like a beat box. The effect was pretty cool. He said that he wanted to be an animator, which made sense. He made a cartoon out of himself. He told me that he made the cartoon, all right, but he wasn't the one who put it on the Internet. In fact, he didn't know who put it on the Internet. The thing that was idiotic about him though was his hair, which looked like a cross between Don King and the drummer from the Jimi Hendrix Experience.

"What's up with that fuckin' hair of yours?" I asked him.

"I don't know," he said. "It's just fucked up, I guess."

"You got any girlfriends out there in Norway?"

"No, I had a really bad girlfriend a couple of years ago."

"Why was she bad?"

"She was just kind of psycho and she pushed me down in shit."

"Maybe she was on high-grade narcotics," I said. "You know, a lot of these women . . . is narcotics legal there in Norway?"

"Yeah, yeah."

"Oh yeah, what can you buy there?"

"You can buy everything, but magic mushrooms grows up there in the forest so I think a lot of people are eating magic mushooms."

I'm thinkin' this might explain the hair.

"Jesus Christ," I said. "No wonder Norway is in the shape it's in. Everybody walking around on magic mushrooms all the time. Let me ask you a question: How are the women over there? Are they a little fast? Is it easy to pick up a girl in Norway?"

"No. They are, what-do-you-call-it, not sluts. They are the opposite of sluts. They are class."

"I'm sorry to hear that. If they're the opposite of sluts I don't want nothin' to do with them. If you buy 'em a cheese-burger and a Coke will they let you sleep with them?" I said.

"No. Class."

"I like sluts. I like classy sluts, too. Listen, the Big Man wants to wish you the best of luck, son."

"Thanks."

I signed off that episode by saying, "Stay tuned next time for more of this shit. What a show!" and I signed on the next episode by saying, "Welcome to Viral Vidiocy, the show where you get to meet some of the Internet's biggest stars. Tonight we get to meet Christian Bagley, star of the Christian Bagley Show. Yeah, I never heard of it, either." Christian lived in the Southwest where, in the summertime, the temperature gets into the hundreds every fuckin' day. His fuckin' jackass shtick was that he put his ass on manhole covers that were out in the sun and purposely burned himself.

"Christian," I asked, "what possesses you to put your ass on a hot, burning manhole cover?"

I could tell by the way Christian spoke that he didn't go to any schools for gifted kids, unless that gift was being fuckin' retarded.

"I do that with my ass because not a lot of people put their asses on manhole covers," Christian said.

What more of a reason do you fuckin' need?

"What was the temperature when you put your ass on the manhole cover?" I asked. Being a trained fucking journalist, I know to keep those questions comin'.

"It was a hundred and eight degrees outside," Christian responded.

"How hot was that manhole cover?"

"I dunno. It was hotter'n hell."

"Could you fry a fuckin' egg on there?"

"Yeah."

"Where is your friend Michael today, the one who put the fuckin' firecracker in his mouth?"

"He couldn't make it. He's at football practice and I guess they kept him for an extra hour."

"Did he ever tell you why he put a firecracker in his mouth?" I asked.

"What a minute. Michael is here right now," Christian said. See, that's the beauty of doing this shit live. The unexpected.

"Breaking news right here!" I said. "Michael just walked in. Can you imagine how lucky I am? Come on, Mike, sit down on the couch there and let me hear what you got to say! Tell me about the firecracker you put in your mouth. Did you blow any teeth out? Come on, I wanna hear. What inspired you to do that?"

Now Christian wasn't a great orator and I wasn't expecting much from Michael, either. Being that he put explosives in his mouth, I figured oral communication might not be his strong point. I wasn't disappointed. Michael spoke like a guy with an infected tongue.

"Well, what happened was, I had a firecracker in my mouth, and I lit it, and it went off, and it went up my nose and it really hurt." Notice that the question, which was "why?" bounced right off of Michael's skull.

"What do you think? Are you trying to be like that Johnny Knockville guy?"

"Yes," Christian chimed in. "We want to be bigger than that, bigger than *Jackass*."

"There it is, ladies and gentlemen, the future of America! All right, Christian, tell me about the show. What's it all about?"

"It's about a group of kids who like to do some stupid shit because there's nothing else to do, you know, and have fun . . ."

I couldn't take it anymore. "Douche bags!" I interjected. "Did it ever occur to you, to you, that you *are* fuckin' stupid? That you *are* fuckin' jackasses?"

There was a pause, tick-tick-tick, then Christian and Michael said, at the same time, "Yesssss." Ah, self-awareness.

My next show put me in touch with some dimwits named Jim, Cletus, and Denny Ray from down there in the state of Arkansas. These guys' claim to fame was that they launched fifteen thousand bottle rockets at the same time.

And while those fuckin' bottle rockets were launching, they hopped up and down on one foot and screamed, "Heeeeeee-yahhhhhhh!" Then they went back to what they usually do, which is smokin' and drinkin' and belchin'.

"So, fellas, tell me, the Big Man has got to know. Just how fuckin' bored do you have to be to blow off fifteen thousand bottle rockets at the same time? Ain't there no fuckin' cows left that need to be tipped? Ain't there no greased pig contest to keep you fuckin' occupied?"

"We just wanted to shoot some bottle rockets, that's all it is," Denny Ray said. "We're amateur rocket scientists. I got a license for . . . uhhhhhh . . . what the hell is it I got a license for?"

"Pyro . . . uhhhhh . . . pyro . . ." said Cletus.

"That's it," Denny Ray said. "I got a license for pyro techniciating."

"This is engineering at its finest," I said. "How come you shot off so many bottle rockets at once?"

"That's just what we do on the Fourth of July," Jim said—and then he let out with a long beer belch.

"The Fourth of July is a very important holiday to us," Cletus chimed in. "It's right up there with Groundhog Day and all them other major ones."

"Hey, Cletus, how long did it take you to get ready to set off all them bottle rockets?" I asked.

"Well," Cletus replied, "it took me about five hours of drinkin' beer and unwrapping bottle rockets, then about two hours of getting everything set up."

"Next year," Denny Ray said, "it's gonna be ever bigger. It's gonna be, uhhhh, large."

"What do you mean, next year?" Cletus asked.

"This year. That's right. This year," Denny Ray said, flashing a grin that, if this was bowling, would have been a really tough spare.

"How important are cigarettes and beer in this process?" I asked.

They didn't say nothin'. They just belched in unison, which answered the question better than words could've, I thought.

"I guess you guys won't be winnin' any safety awards any time soon, huh?" I asked.

"I been criticized for smokin' around this stuff," Cletus said. "Just to show that it ain't dangerous I'm gonna throw a cigarette into that box right there, a full case of bottle rockets, and you'll see that there ain't nothing to worry about."

That was what he did. In about five seconds, the whole fuckin' box blew up like a fuckin' hand grenade had gone off.

"Holy shit!" I said. "I ain't never seen nothin' like that. That was great, fellas!"

"Come on down here to Arkansas," Jim said, signing off. "I'll hook you up with my cousin."

"Wanna touch my sister?" Cletus added.

"What a show!" I screamed.

That's the shit I been doing. I didn't get my big shot with a sitcom yet but I'm still hopeful. You never know. I could be the next fuckin' Kramer.

> *"Leprychauns don't take no crack,"* Shawn said. *"We get drunk and we get high but other than that we don't smoke no crack."*

## Pete the Nut

A lot of people on the street been comin' up to me and tellin' me how much they liked my first book. They say they like the rantin' and the ravin', but their favorite part is when I talk about the good old days, growing up in fuckin' Canarsie.

Now back in them days we used to have a guy in the old neighborhood called Pete the Nut. The name didn't come from the number of testicles he had or anything like that. It came because this guy had a screw loose.

The balcony was closed, if you know what I'm fuckin' saying. He didn't get that way because he fell on his head or because someone cracked open his skull with a fuckin' baseball bat. He was born with a fuckin' faulty attic.

I swear on my mother, this story is true. I was fourteen, fifteen years old and Pete the Nut—who was older and was already doin' some work for some people—came up to me and said, "Big Mike, let me take you out for a good Italian dinner."

I like to eat, so I said, "Lead the way."

So Pete the Nut took me to Rizzo's Pizzeria over there on

Rockaway Parkway and Glenwood Road. We went in there and we ate like fuckin' horses. We started out with baked clams, just the fuckin' appetizer.

Then we ordered two huge plates of linguine with fuckin' clam sauce, then all kinds of fuckin' desserts. After a couple of fuckin' hours, when we were finally done eating, the waiter brought the check.

I swear on my mother, Pete the Nut took one look at the check, threw his head back so his fuckin' face was pointed at the ceiling, and howled like a fuckin' wolf. You'd've thought he was fuckin' Lon Chaney Jr.

"Ahhhhhhhh-WOOOOOOOOOOO!" he howled. And then he did it again, and again, and again. I'm lookin' at 'em like this fucking guy has lost whatever mind he fuckin' had in the first place. But there was method in his fuckin' madness.

The waiter got the manager and the manager got the owner and the owner fuckin' said, "Get the fuck out of here." I swear, true story. We ate and ate and ate and when the check came, we didn't pay a fuckin' dime. Pete the Nut just kept on howling until they tossed our asses out of there.

Lookin' back on it, I'm surprised more fuckers ain't tried that. You go into a fancy restaurant, work up a five-hundred-dollar tab, and then howl until you get booted back out onto the street. After all, is it fuckin' illegal to howl?

> *I swear on my mother, Pete the Nut took one look at the check, threw his head back so his fuckin' face was pointed at the ceiling, and howled like a fuckin' wolf.*

## Two Kinds of People the Big Man Can't Stand

People are always askin' me, hey Big Man, what kind of people don't you like? Now I am not a hateful man. I'm not the kind of guy who goes around hating people, but there are two kinds of people I can't stand.

The first are cheap bastards. I can't stand 'em. These are the fuckin' misers out there, the fuckin' people who wouldn't even give their mother a fuckin' Mother's Day card on Mother's Day. Too expensive.

Now, if you're poor and you can't afford shit, that's one thing, but the folks that got it but don't want to spend it, they really burn me up, the cheap cocksuckers. They're rollin' in it, but they ain't fuckin' parting with it. They want to take it with them into their fuckin' graves.

Number two: The Big Man can't stand people who don't fuckin' take care of their body. These are the dirty, smelly people. I can't stand these motherfuckers. A bar of fuckin' soap only costs fifty-nine cents. Get the fuck out of here. Go home and take a fuckin' bath, you cocksuckers.

So now you know. I hate cheap, fuckin' dirty bastards. So if you're a cheap, fuckin' dirty bastard, I hate you fuckin' guys.

> *A bar of fuckin' soap only costs fifty-nine cents. Get the fuck out of here. Go home and take a fuckin' bath, you cocksuckers.*

## Little Tony the Wop

I got a friend of mine from back in the old days, we call him Little Tony the Wop. Not too long ago, Tony the Wop almost committed suicide, almost drank himself to death. He didn't come out of the house for almost a month.

You want to know why he was so depressed? He got caught eatin' in one of them Olive Gardens. If I ever got caught eatin' in a fuckin' Olive Garden, I'd take a fuckin' rope and I'd fuckin' hang myself.

What a fuckin' poison pit. Olive Garden tastes worse than that Franco-American spaghetti and meatballs. It's a real fuckin' shithole. So here's a word to the wise to you fuckin' real Italians out there: Don't get caught eatin' in a fuckin' Olive Garden.

*You want to know why he was so depressed? He got caught eatin' in one of them Olive Gardens.*

## Why I Still Hate Cell Phones

Now, I've already told you how I hate cell phones, and I still do, more than ever. It makes the Big Man want to sing, "I hate cell phones more today than yesterday, but not as much as tomorrow." I tell ya, it's a big fuckin' problem in this country today.

Everywhere you go, they ring in about a hundred different tones. You could be standin' in line at the fuckin' post office or maybe in a fuckin' bank and, the next thing you fuckin' know, it sounds like you're in a fuckin' arcade.

You got "The Star-Spangled Banner," you got blues music, you got rap music, you got that teeny bopper music that Disney cranks out. It's turning the fuckin' world into a cacophony of noise. I was in a restaurant the other day and about five cell phones went off at one fuckin' time.

RING! RING! I was tryin' to sit there and fuckin' relax and eat a fuckin' meal. But you can't do it in this day and age because of all the fuckin' cell phones going off. The worst is when you get fuckin' old people with a cell phone. They don't even know how to work the fuckin' thing.

They pick it up and go, "HELLO! HELLO! I FUCKIN' CAN'T HEAR YOU!"

Finally, I got fuckin' aggravated and I left the fuckin' table and went into the men's room. I'm sittin' on the bowl. All I want to do is take a fuckin' dump in peace. I'm in there for two minutes when RING! RING! You can't even take a fuckin' shit these days without cell phones goin' off all around you.

There ought to be a fuckin' law against these fuckin' cell phones. They go off in movie theaters when you're tryin' to watch the fuckin' picture. RING! RING! I feel like hittin' the fuckin' guy over the head with a fuckin' baseball bat.

Whatever happened to fuckin' phone booths? You go in there, you close the door, and you talk in fuckin' privacy. Whatever happened to them? They're fuckin' extinct.

*The worst is when you get fuckin' old people with a cell phone. They don't even know how to work the fuckin' thing.*

## Trying to Get Ointment for My Balls

One of my favorite sayings is: "The fuckin' world is comin' to an end." Well, I went into a CVS the other day and the pharmacist was an Indian. You know, they don't hire Americans no more. Don't get me wrong. I got nothin' against Indian people. Believe me, I got nothin' against 'em.

So it was an Indian woman. She came over to me and said, "May I help you, sir?"

I said, "Yes, I'd like one male urinal and the strongest ointment you got for jock itch."

She looked at me and she said, "I'm so sorry, sir. I don't understand what you're saying."

I said, "I want a male urinal. I gotta piss. I need something I can piss in."

Then she knew. I could see her fuckin' eyes light up. She said, "So sorry, sir. I understand."

"And I need something for jock itch. I need something real strong for jock itch."

She said, "Excuse me, sir. I don't understand. What exactly is jock itch?"

I said, "My fuckin' balls are itching!" I started scratching myself. I had to show her the fuckin' problem. Then she knew. I'm fuckin' standing there and my fuckin' balls were on fire. My fuckin' balls were itching me like a fuckin' son of a bitch and this fuckin' woman didn't know what fuckin' jock itch was.

*She said, "Excuse me, sir. I don't understand. What exactly is jock itch?"*

## The First Time

Heyyyyyyyy, all you readers, remember the first time? Everybody remembers the first time. I remember the first time I . . . ejaculated. I was in the Canarsie Theater. I went to the movies with six kids and my friend's older sister.

Her name was Marissa Falcone and she was seventeen years old. She was just seventeen if you know what I mean, and, take my fuckin' word for it, the way she looked was way beyond fuckin' compare.

I was only thirteen and she sat right alongside me as I was watching an Elvis Presley movie. It was called *Love Me Tender*. Yes, it was. I was eating some popcorn and I was drinkin' a soda.

Marissa Falcone put her hand on my leg and, the next thing I knew, I got a surprise. Something started to rise. She started rubbin'. Nice and easy. Then harder and harder. And, all of a sudden . . .

Pop went the weasel!

And she looked at me and she said, "Did that feel nice?"

And I said, "It sure did! Let's do it again."

And I did it four more times, right there in the movie theater. I remember that day like it was yesterday.

I remember the first time I got stoned. I drank a quart of anisette, you know that shit that tastes like licorice. True, I got fuckin' stoned, but I threw up my fuckin' guts for five fuckin' days. It was one day of pukin' and four more of dry heavin'.

I never wanted to see a bottle of anisette again. I ain't had a shot of anisette or a piece of licorice in over forty-five fuckin' years. That's how fuckin' sick I got. I don't even fuckin' want to smell licorice.

I remember the first time I smoked a reefer. I wanna tell ya, I got high as a fuckin' kite. Later on, I went home and I ate my mother out of house and fuckin' home. I ate everything in fuckin' sight.

My mother said, "Michael, what's wrong with you? You're eating everything."

I said, "I'm starvin', Ma. I'm fuckin' starvin'."

So take some time, dear readers, and think about some of your first times. Makes me want to sing, "Feeeeels like the first time. Feeeels like the very first time!"

> *I was only thirteen and she sat right alongside me as I was watching an Elvis Presley movie. It was called* Love Me Tender. *Yes, it was.*

## Confucius Say

One of my ancient mentors is the Chinese philosopher Confucius. Here are some of my favorite proverbs from this Chinese master:

Confucius say, woman who suck cock swallow heavy load. Confucius say.

Confucius say, man who eats pussy always makes woman go meow. Confucius say.

Confucius say, man with huge balls always carries big pistol. Confucius say.

Confucius say, show me woman who travels both ways, I show you Senator Hillary Clinton. Confucius say.

Confucius say, man who pisses in dark always misses bowl. Confucius say.

Confucius say, man who eats too much born with two assholes. Confucius say.

Confucius say, show me man who never had sexual relations with that woman, I show you ex-president Bill Clinton. Confucius say.

Confucius say, show me man who say if I did it, I show you O. J. Simpson. Confucius say.

Confucius say, show me man with brain the size of pea, I show you President George W. Bush. Confucius say.

Confucius say, show me man who cannot even shoot straight, I show you Vice President Dick Cheney. Confucius say.

Confucius say, show me rice that man cannot eat, I show you Condoleezza Rice. Confucius say.

Confucius say, show me one rich man, I show you the thousands of men he stole from. Confucius say.

Confucius say, show me man with one hair on head fifteen miles long and I show you Donald Trump. Confucius say.

Confucius say, none can deny that the greatest fool of all is he who lives poor so he can die rich. Confucius say.

Confucius say, man who seeks funny ice skate seeks gay blade. Confucius say.

Confucius say, show me woman who inhales food and exhales shit, I show you Rosie O'Donnell. Confucius say.

Confucius say, man who can't find hole is lost. Confucius say.

Confucius say, beware of man who is politician, for he will always blow smoke up your ass. Confucius say.

Confucius say, man who fucks Chinese woman is horny one hour later. Confucius say.

Confucius say, man who kisses ass always have shitty lips. Confucius say.

Confucius say, man who go to bed with itchy asshole wake up with stink finger. Confucius say.

Confucius say, man who seek Osama bin Laden is blind. Confucius say.

Confucius say, man with long tongue needs no cock. Confucius say.

Confucius say, show me tightwad, I show you Bill O'Reilly. Confucius say.

Confucius say, show me man who speaks through asshole, again I show you Bill O'Reilly. Confucius say.

Confucius say, show me man who has sex with many women at same time, I show you one happy motherfucker. Confucius say.

Confucius say, show me woman who is bald both on top and on bottom, I show you Britney Spears. Confucius say.

Confucius say, show me woman who has lost both panties and children, again I show you Britney Spears. Confucius say.

Confucius say, show me woman who like to lick stick, I show you Paris Hilton. Confucius say.

Confucius say, show me older man who marries younger woman, I show you older man who uses Viagra. Confucius say.

Confucius say, the world is fuckin' comin' to an end. Confucius say.

One more, one fuckin' more: Confucius say, show me Chinese hooker, I show you woman who'll sell crack. Confucius say.

Confucius say, Big Man always happy to see you.

*Confucius say, man who kisses ass always have shitty lips.*

## Getting Laid for Free

You know, I feel sorry for the young fellas today. They got to take young women out on expensive dates, drop a coupla hundred bucks, winin' and dinin' 'em. It was different back in my day, let me tell you.

Back in the good old days, you asked a broad out, all ya had to do was take her to a pizzeria for a slice of pizza, take her to a movie, and then, if you were lucky, you'd get a little touch, you'd get a little feel, you'd get a little kiss.

Today, these young women make guys spend all their green. They want to be taken to fancy restaurants. They want to drive around in $60,000 cars. They want to sit front row at some sold-out show.

A guy today has a tough time. But I got to tell you fellas, take it from the ol' Big Man, you got it all wrong. I was on that Sirius radio the other day. I was on station 198, a station that put the "Blue" in "Blue Planet."

The language they were using on that station made me sound like a fuckin' choirboy. So I don't want anybody to complain about the language that the Big Man uses. Just go on that Playboy station. They make me sound like a Cub Scout.

So you fellas out there who can't afford to take out these women with their expensive tastes, don't worry about it. There are plenty of women out there. The Earth is crawlin' with them, and they are fast today.

I'll tell you why you got it made. Twenty-five percent of the men out there are gay. Another 30 or 40 percent are fucked up on alcohol and drugs. So that leaves a limited number of straight guys out there. The women outnumber us ten to fuckin' one.

So, you fuckin' single guys, get out there and go to work. Leave your fuckin' wallet in your pocket. Just say, "I'm straight and I'm sober," and the fuckin' women will be so fast you'll think they're fuckin' race car drivers.

They want to go quick, you know what I'm sayin'? What do you think, they don't want a hotshot? So get out there and get it for nothin'. Take 'em out for a cheeseburger and a Coke. That should be enough.

Boy, I'll never forget the good old days back there in Brooklyn when I was fifteen, sixteen years old sitting in the backseat of a car with a girl, trying to get her to "go all the way." While I was kissin' her and I had my tongue down her throat, I'd put my hand on her shoulder.

I used to slide that hand down, down, down, just to see how far I could get. Finally my hand would get to her tit and then I'd work my hand up under her bra and I'd be feelin' her tit. Then, if I had enough balls, I'd go down to her thighs.

I'd work my hand up her legs and get a feel of her bush. And if she didn't squawk, I'd get her fuckin' panties down all the way past her knees and, I want to tell you, that was scorin' a fuckin' home run.

Today, it's another fuckin' ball game. No challenge getting the panties off a woman today. Take that Britney Spears. What's the fun in makin' out with fuckin' Britney Spears? She's

shaved off her fuckin' bush—not even a fuckin' soul patch—
and her panties are already off.

That's the way it is with these women today. Their drawers are already pulled down! They want you to get in there
and give it to 'em. I tell ya, you young fellas got it easy today.
Back in my time back in Brooklyn, they called it, "going all
the fuckin' way," and it was quite a fuckin' journey gettin' there.

**Brad Pitt? George Clooney? Guess again. This is me. Look real
long at this picture cause I don't smile much. (photo courtesy
Mrs. Kid from Brooklyn)**

*What's the fun in makin' out with fuckin' Britney Spears? She's shaved off her fuckin' bush and her panties are already off.*

## Albert Sardi vs. Ralph the Cop

I got to laugh. I was thinkin' back the other day, back to the old days when I was fifteen, sixteen years old, and we used to go over there to Samuel J. Tillman High School, which was in the East Flatbush section of Brooklyn.

I had a friend back then named Albert Sardi. He was a stringy guy. He was about six foot, tipped the scaled at one forty, soakin' wet. Stringy. But, I got to tell you, he was a great fuckin' fighter. Quick hands. Deceptive power. I'd put Albert up against anybody.

Then we had a guy walked a beat around the school, named Ralph the Cop. He was a big fuckin' husky guy. He was built. One day, Sardi went up to Ralph the Cop and said, "I don't think you're so fuckin' tough. Take that fuckin' gun and badge off and I'll show you."

And it was on. Ralph the Cop took off his fuckin' gun and badge and, wouldn't you know it, fuckin' Sardi ripped into him. You could see the way it was gonna go right away. Sardi was too quick. Ralph was clumsy, useless. His punches were slow, telegraphed, and by the time they got there, Albert was someplace else. Sardi tore the fuckin' shit out of him. When Sardi was done with him, Ralph the Cop was layin' there on the fuckin' floor, fuckin' cryin'.

So the next time you're in Vegas or talkin' to a fuckin' bookie and you want to bet the fights, here's a word to the wise. The guy who looks the fuckin' toughest don't always win. It's the guy who's got fast hands and the guy who knows how to fuckin' duck who wins the fight, and that was stringy ol' Albert Sardi.

> *When Sardi was done with him, Ralph the Cop was layin' there on the fuckin' floor, fuckin' cryin'.*

## How to Blow Off Telemarketers

You ever get up, eight, eight thirty in the morning, go into the bathroom, start brushing your teeth, and the next thing you know, RING! RING! So you run out to answer the fuckin' phone, almost break a fuckin' leg, and it's one of them tele-marketers.

I hate them fuckin' cocksuckers. They ought to give them fuckin' cocksuckers fines. They shouldn't be allowed to fuckin' call you. The first time, they should get a $500 fuckin' fine. The second time, they should get fuckin' six months in jail. The third time: three fuckin' years.

What do they got to bother you for? You come home at seven o'clock at night after a hard day's work, you're trying to watch the fuckin' news on television, and the phone goes RING! RING! RING!

"Hello, Mr. Caracciolo. I'm calling from . . ."

"Go fuck yourself! I don't fuckin' want to be bothered."

Click. Sure it feels good to tell 'em to go fuck themselves

and it gets rid of 'em on the short term, but they're like cockroaches after the bomb, they keep coming back.

So I got a new way of doin' it now. I'm gonna teach you readers how to do it, too. Every time you get a telemarketer on the phone, here's what you do: as soon as you hear the caller's voice, you go like this: "OOOOH, DIIIIII, WAHHHHHH-HHHH. OOOOOOOH, DIIIIIIIII, WAAAAAHHHH!"

Once they hear it's a fuckin' Chinaman, their gonna hang right up on you. And they ain't gonna call back. There's no fuckin' doubt about it. There's not a fuckin' salesman on the fuckin' Earth who can sell a fuckin' Chinaman a stick of chewing gum. That's the tip of the day. Believe me, it works 100 percent of the time.

> *There's not a fuckin' salesman on the fuckin' Earth who can sell a fuckin' Chinaman a stick of chewing gum.*

## People Got Their Priorities All Fucked Up

You know, it's a funny thing about human nature. A guy goes to a casino, gives his wife $200, and says, "Here, honey, go play the slots. I'm goin' over to play some blackjack and craps."

He walks away. He loses two, three thousand shooting craps and playing blackjack. Goes back and meets his wife; says, "How'd you do, honey?"

"I lost," she says in a whiny voice.

"Yeah, all right," the guy says. "Let's get out of here."

"But I'm hungry," she says. "I wanna get something to eat."

He says, "The food's too expensive here. We can't eat in here. Let's go outside."

The fuckin' guy just lost two, three thousand dollars and he's telling his wife it's too expensive to eat in the casino. So he winds up going outside, goin' to a fuckin' Burger King or a fuckin' McDonald's or even eatin' fuckin' hot dogs off a fuckin' cart. He's eatin' garbage food off the street.

Then there's the guy who goes out and pays $300 for a bag of snuff. You know, he wants to get all coked up. He's got a fuckin' date, so he goes to the guy out on the street (that's me) and says he needs two tickets for Madonna.

"I got two front row center," I says.

"How much are they, pal?" he asks.

"Three hundred each," I say.

"Three hundred each? What are you, crazy?"

Am I crazy? Am I crazy? The guy just spent $300 on coke and sniffed it up his fuckin' nose. And he's worried about spending the money on a fuckin' ticket—but that's the way people are today. For their fuckin' bad habits, they'll pay any fuckin' thing. For something good, they don't wanna pay.

> *The fuckin' guy just lost two, three thousand and he's telling his wife it's too expensive to eat in the casino.*

## The F Word Is a Mighty Fine Word

The Big Man gets between two and three thousand e-mails a day. I noticed a lot of people complain about my language.

They say I use the f word too often. You know the f word, right? F-U-C-K. *Fuck.*

*Fuck* is a common word. It's used by hundreds of millions of people every day. For instance, imagine you are an attorney and you just found out the prosecution has got a surprise witness. You go over and tell your client, "I think we're fucked!"

Or a guy asks ya, "Say, how's the food in that restaurant?" You say, "It's fuckin' great!"

Or, if you don't like somebody, you tell him, "Go fuck yourself."

Or, if you're lookin' to score on this broad, you go up to her and say, "Boy, would I like to fuck you."

The word is great. It's versatile. It's used in thirty, forty different ways. It's a fuckin' common word. So all of you people out there who don't like the word F-U-C-K, I got one thing to tell you:

Go fuck yourself, you fuckin' rat bastard!

**Fuck** *is a common word. It's used by hundreds of millions of people every day.*

## The Real Meaning of the Word *Pimp*

For all you people out there who are wondering the meaning of the word *pimp*, the Big Man has got all of the answers for you. Most people think that a pimp is just a guy who prostitutes women. But a real fuckin' pimp, he prostitutes everybody.

A pimp is a fuckin' taker. A fuckin' user. A pimp wouldn't give the sweat off his own fuckin' balls to his own fuckin' mother. He only knows how to fuckin' take. If you're down on your fuckin' back lying on the fuckin' ground, a fuckin' pimp'll come over and stick a fuckin' knife in ya. That's what a fuckin' pimp is.

And most guys that I fuckin' know are fuckin' pimps. I was lying down on my fuckin' back. I was fuckin' struggling. I needed help. But not one fuckin' cocksucker that I know helped me.

You know why? They're fuckin' pimps. They're fuckin' takers. They're no fuckin' good. They'd fuck their own mother. I hate your fuckin' guts, you rotten fuckin' pimps. And you know who the fuck you are.

Lose my fuckin' number, you evil bastards, you rotten son of a bitches. Rot in hell, you cocksucker pimps!

---

*A pimp is a fuckin' taker. A fuckin' user. A pimp woudn't give the sweat off his own fuckin' balls to his own fuckin' mother.*

---

## How Do You Fuck Up Toast?

You know, I'm fuckin' steamed. I just got back from the fuckin' diner. The thing that's got me frosted is toast. It seems like such a simple thing. Fuckin' toast. You put the fuckin' bread in the toaster, it pops up, and you give it to the customer.

How the fuck can you fuck that up? But they can. Today, I got my toast, it was fuckin' cold as ice. It was fuckin' colder than the bread was before it got fuckin' toasted. How the fuck is that even possible?

The other thing about toast that pisses me off is the butter. Now, there was a time back in the old days when the fuckin' toast came with butter on it. Today, they give you these little fuckin' butter packets and you got to struggle just to get the fuckin' things open.

Then when you finally got the fuckin' butter packet open, you go in there with a knife and the butter is fuckin' hard as a rock. Then you try to spread the fuckin' hard butter on the fuckin' icy toast and it's the end of the fuckin' world.

So I ordered fuckin' French toast. Again, you'd think pretty simple, right? I had to send the fuckin' thing back three times because it came out fuckin' raw. Where the fuck do they get these short-order cooks from, fuckin' Siberia? Where the fuck do they come from?

Finally, I get the fuckin' French toast cooked right and I go to put the fuckin' syrup on and, you guessed it, I got another fuckin' packet to open up. This one's even harder than the fuckin' butter to get open and you end up with the fuckin' syrup all over your fuckin' fingers.

By the time I got the fuckin' syrup on the French toast, it was fuckin' cold. I fuckin' quit.

*Then when you finally got the fuckin' butter packet open, you go in there with a knife and the butter is fuckin' hard as a rock.*

# Take My Word for It, Fellas, the Meter Is Always Running

You know, I've known for years that women were funny. Not fuckin' ha-ha funny. They're odd. They're a very peculiar species, women. You ever read a personal ad written by a woman? They always say the same fuckin' thing: "I'm looking for a man who is financially secure."

There it is. They want the fuckin' money. Guys put an ad in the paper because they're lonely or horny or whatever. Women put an ad in the fuckin' paper it's always for the same fuckin' reason: they want the fuckin' cash.

I was in Atlantic City the other night, stayin' in a hotel, and the walls, they were a little bit on the thin side. I could hear every fuckin' thing that was goin' on in the next room. And there was fuckin' goin' on.

This guy was fuckin' this fuckin' broad and I want to tell you, he was workin'. Maybe he had a few shots of whiskey in him or something, but he was workin', pumpin' away like a fuckin' jackhammer over there.

He must've been sweatin' bullets and I can hear her urging him on, "Fuck me! Fuck me!"

I was worried about the fuckin' guy. I thought he was going to bust a nut or something over there, on account of the fuckin' workout she was giving him. It was the kind of fuck that can make a guy's toes fuckin' fall off.

And, I swear to God, she was goin', "I saw these pair of shoes downstairs . . ." He was pumpin' and the bed was squeakin' and they were both breathing like it was the ninth quarter of a fuckin' basketball game. "They cost seven hundred dollars a pair," she said. Pump, pump, pump. Moan, groan. "And they look so good on me," she said.

And he was goin', "Yeah, baby. Yeah, baby. I'll buy 'em for you, baby."

The guy hadn't even blown his fuckin' wad yet and she was telling him she wanted a fuckin' pair of shoes. That's fuckin' broads for ya. I'll tell you, if that had been me over in that room fuckin' that broad and I was workin' so hard and fuckin' sweatin' bullets on account of I was fuckin' her so hard and she started talking about fuckin' shoes, I wanna tell ya, my fuckin' dick would have gone fuckin' limp. How the fuck can you keep your fuckin' cock hard when the fuckin' broad is asking for $700 shoes right in the middle of the fuck?

Anyway, that's the way women are today. Fuck, that's the way everybody fuckin' is today. Gimme, gimme, gimme. They want fuckin' money. You want to make some friends quick? Just go out with a fuckin' wheelbarrow full of fuckin' money and start handin' it out. You'll have plenty of fuckin' friends. Everybody wants money. They don't want to work for it. They want it given to them.

*The guy hadn't even blown his fuckin' wad yet and she was telling him she wanted a fuckin' pair of shoes. That's fuckin' broads for ya.*

## Old-Fashioned Melting-Pot Vocabulary

Back in the old days, back in Brooklyn, you had a lot of fuckin' nationalities all living together. And we all had names for one another, just to rub it up everyone's ass. If you were

Italian like me, you got called a greaseball. Or a wop. Or a dago.

If you were a Jew, you got called a Heeb, or a kike. If you were Chinese, they called you a Chink. If you were Irish, you got called a Mick. If you were Spanish, they called you a spic. The Germans got called Krauts. Everybody had a name.

Then there were the blacks. They must have had thirty fuckin' different names. There were more words meaning "black" than there were meaning "drunk." Now I swear to my mother that I am not a prejudiced guy when I say this.

They were moonyans, schitzus, niggers, spearchuckers, spooks, eggplants, shines, jungle bunnies . . . Must have been thirty names. I gotta tell ya, I felt sorry for the poor bastards.

Back then, you'd run into somebody didn't like you, he'd say, "Get the fuck out of here you fuckin' Heeb wop. You fuckin' Mick cocksucker, I'll cut your fuckin' balls off."

That's the way it was in the early fifties in Brooklyn.

*There were more words meaning "black" than there were meaning "drunk."*

## Where Did All the Americans Go?

I gotta tell ya, I feel like a fuckin' foreigner in my own fuckin' country. Here's a tip: Don't ever go into a gas station and ask for directions. The people that work in the fuckin' gas station don't even speak English and, even if they did, they don't know where the fuck they are much less where the fuck you want to go.

You say, "Where the fuck is Mackay Place?" and they say, "Abbaabbaabba, hommahommahomma."

You go into one of these fast-food joints today and it's all fuckin' foreigners in there. I can't understand one fuckin' word they say. "Abbaabbaabba, hommahommahomma." What the fuck is that? You order something, they get it fuckin' wrong.

You go into a fuckin' diner and it's the same fuckin' thing. I can't even understand the bastards and they sure as shit don't understand me. Where are the American people? I don't see 'em around no more.

Where did they go? Where did all the fuckin' Americans go? I tell ya, it doesn't matter where the fuck you go, they're speakin' another fuckin' language. Who knows what the fuck they're speaking?

*Where are the American people?*
*I don't see 'em around no more.*

## Weddings

The Big Man wants to tell you about weddings. You remember weddings? That's the greatest fuckin' day in the bride's life and the worst day in the groom's. She's been planning for fuckin' months and she's wearing a gown that cost more money than your grandfather's house.

He's hungover and hasn't been to sleep. His hair isn't even fuckin' combed and he is hoping he doesn't fuckin' puke while he's takin' the fuckin' vows.

Now, all weddings are pretty much the same no matter what ethnicity you are, but there are differences, and here's one that I noticed.

You go to a Jewish wedding today and all of the envelopes are a little thin. That's because everyone writes a fuckin' check. You go to an Italian wedding and the envelopes are an inch and a half thick. All cash. Cash money.

I had a friend of mine, Tommy Funzi from the Bronx. When he got married, they had to hire two armed guards to walk him and his bride out of the reception because of all the fuckin' cash they were carrying. They must have walked out of that reception hall with a half-million dollars, and I ain't fuckin' shittin' with you—and every fuckin' cent of it was in cash.

> **When Tommy Funzi got married, they had to hire two armed guards to walk him and his bride out of the reception because of all the fuckin' cash they were carrying.**

## What to Do with the Mexicans

Every night on the fuckin' news, you hear about the problems we got here in America on account of the Mexicans pouring across the border. There are, like, a million fuckin'

Mexicans crossing the border every day. Tens of millions are already here. What should we do? What the fuck should we do? That's what they're sayin' on the fuckin' news.

Well, the Big Man is here to tell you that these newspeople got the wrong fuckin' idea. The Mexicans are doing us a fucking favor by coming here. They do all the jobs that Americans don't want to do.

There's a simple solution to this so-called problem. Listen to the Big Man, now. You take all the Mexicans and you let 'em build the highways. You let 'em build all the roads. You let 'em dig all the fuckin' ditches.

The Americans aren't gonna do it, and even if you could find any fuckin' Americans who would do it, they would all belong to some fuckin' union and they'd take twenty fuckin' years doing a job that could be done in three fuckin' months.

It's common sense. With all of these fuckin' labor unions today, these guys are making thirty, forty fuckin' dollars an hour to dig fuckin' ditches and build the fuckin' roads. And the job never gets done fuckin' right. You ever have trouble gettin' to fuckin' work in the morning because there's construction going on on the road? They rip up the road, do whatever the fuck it is that they got to do, pave it back up again, and, ooops, they forgot to do something so they got to rip the fuckin' thing up all over again and do it again. Everybody gets over-fuckin'-paid twice for one fuckin' job. That's the way it is today.

Now, I know they say the fuckin' tortoise beats the fuckin' hare, but these guys out there workin' with their big labor-union paychecks, they don't work like tortoises. They couldn't handle that kind of fuckin' pace. These guys work so slow that a fuckin' snail could beat them.

So you bring in the Mexicans who came here to work, and that's the fuckin' reason they're comin' here, 'cause there ain't no fuckin' jobs down in fuckin' Mexico, and you give 'em all these fuckin' job that Americans don't want, or the jobs it's costing us taxpayers an arm and a leg to pay for.

I mean, let's get real, there are a lot of fuckin' highways out there with a lot of fuckin' potholes to get fixed. And we don't just need to fix the old roads, we need to build new roads, too. There's all kinds of fucking excavation that the fuckin' Mexicans can do, and we wouldn't have to pay 'em anywhere near thirty, forty fuckin' bucks an hour. Fuck, a lot of 'em would be glad to put in a full day's work in exchange for a fuckin' box lunch.

Here's the deal we give 'em. They come over here and they work for three years, building new highways or excavating the land or whatever the fuck it is that needs to be done, and after the three years we give them citizenship. Everybody fuckin' wins.

As long as they show that they are hard working, that they're fuckin' honest, and they want to stay here, give 'em the fuckin' job. Let 'em do it. Because, face it, the Americans don't want to do it, and you know why? Because we are a fucking lazy people, that's why. We want every fuckin' thing done for us.

Including me. Don't get me wrong. I ain't no fuckin' angel. I'm just as lazy as the next American. You tell me to go dig a fuckin' ditch and I would tell you to go fuck yourself, you rat bastard.

*Here's the deal: They work for three years, building new highways or excavating the land or whatever the fuck it is that needs to be done, and after the three years we give them citizenship.*

# An American in Paris

You know, Paris Hilton has been famous for a while now. She's got her own perfume and she had her own TV show. She has been in movies and she does, as they fuckin' say, the talk-show circuit. She went to jail and she got out, and then she went to jail again and she got out, and the whole time the paparazzi had their cameras shoved in her face, lookin' for the money shot.

Well, after all that fame, I think it's time to flash back in time and recall the reason that Paris Hilton became famous in the first place. She made a porno movie.

She and her boyfriend at the time, who the fuck knows or fuckin' cares what the fuck his name is, they got out the old camcorder so they could make a movie of this guy pourin' the pork into Paris. She's suckin' the guy's dick and gigglin' and yellin' and laughin'. Holy shit. Can you imagine the poor girl's grandfather or great-grandfather or whatever the fuck he was, Conrad Hilton? A man of honor. He's up there in Heaven, you know. All them rich people, they get to take their servants with them when they go.

He's got the butler and the maid up there with them. The butler probably came up to him and said, "Massa Hilton, your great-granddaughter down there, she's made a film in which she is performin' fellatio."

*"What's that, Leroy? What did you say? My great-granddaughter, Paris, is performing fellatio?"*

And Conrad said, "What's that, Leroy? What did you say? My great-granddaughter, Paris, is performing fellatio?" And then he just rolled over and lay right down, thinkin', Look who I left $300 million to: a fuckin' douche bag.

That's the way the world is today. Nobody got no fuckin' respect no more. There's no more men of honor. People got no fuckin' respect for each other. Nobody's proud no more. Nothin'. That's what it is today.

## You Got to Be Crazy to Be a Cop Today

Take a guy who wants to be a cop today. I say to him, "What are you, out of your fuckin' mind? You don't want to be a fuckin' cop."

They should give cops $200,000 a year to start. You'd have to be fuckin' nuts to be a cop today. You got to go there and you got guys smokin' crack pipes. You got guys shootin' heroin in their arm. Guys smokin' them fuckin' mushrooms. Stoned out of their fuckin' mind, takin' that fuckin' Ecstasy. They'd pull out a fuckin' gun and shoot you in a minute.

Same thing with a fireman. They go whereever the fire is. They run into burnin' buildings. Give them $250,000 a year— to start! Those poor fuckin' bastards deserve every fuckin' penny of it.

They go into a burning building carrying a shitload of equipment, climb up six fuckin' flights of stairs, and then carry down a two-hundred-and-fuckin'-fifty-pound woman to save her fuckin' life.

I'd say, "Fuck you, lady. They ain't payin' me enough moolah to carry you down no fuckin' stairs."

Pay the cops and the firemen more money!

> *They go into a burning building carrying a shitload of equipment, climb up six fuckin' flights of stairs, and then carry down a two-hundred-and-fuckin'-fifty-pound woman to save her fuckin' life.*

## Today, Everything Has Got to Be Fancy

Anybody who's ever visited my Web site (www.kidfrom brooklyn.com, and remember the Big Man is always happy to see ya) knows how I feel about that Starbucks, with their fuckin' five-dollar cups of fuckin' coffeelike drink.

They got their Caffé Mocha and their Cappuccino and their Caffé Latte and all that shit. It's coffee with some steamed milk and maybe a little squirt of syrup—banana, strawberry, whatever they do—and they're chargin' a fuckin' finsky for it. It comes out of a fuckin' blender like a fuckin' smoothie and maybe they put a shot of whipped cream on the top.

But Starbucks is just one fuckin' symptom of what's wrong with the world today—and what's wrong with the world today is that the fuckin' world is comin' to a fuckin' end. Take fuckin' hot dogs.

I went into a gourmet hot dog joint the other day. The guy said, what kind of hot dog you want? I said, whatcha got? He said, we got bacon, we got filet mignon tips, we got sautéed onions and fresh tomatoes. And they charged for the toppings.

By the time you're done payin' for all the toppings, they're chargin' you five dollars for a fuckin' hot dog. Just give me a hot dog with mustard and sauerkraut! I like it the old-fashioned way.

But today everything has got to be fancy. Put this on there. Put that on there. You go to a pancake joint today and you tell 'em you just want a stack of fuckin' pancakes, and they look at you like you got two heads.

They got fifty fuckin' kinds of pancakes and they want to know which kind you want. Just a stack? Doesn't compute with them. Then, once you fuckin' pick what kind of pancakes you want, there's another hundred different kinds of syrups.

I mean, come on! Just give me some maple syrup on a stack of fucking pancakes. That's all I want. I don't want any of this other garbage. I don't give a flying fuck about your hundred different flavors. I just want a stack with some maple syrup, the old-fashioned way. You know what I'm talking about. With a lot of butter.

The thing I hate most about everybody trying to be so fucking fancy today is they think it gives them the fucking excuse to charge fancy prices. Five fuckin' bucks for a cup of coffee. Five fuckin' bucks for a hot dog. The Big Man don't go in for that shit. He goes in for the old-time way.

*You go to a pancake joint today and you tell 'em you just want a stack of fuckin' pancakes, and they look at you like you got two heads.*

# Slow News Days

The Big Man hates to watch the news. I never liked watchin' the fuckin' news much, but now it's fuckin' excruciating. The news is very negative today. Somebody is always getting murdered. Some house is always burning down. Whatever it is. Very negative shit on the news.

But that's not the part that pisses me off. Bad things happen to people and everybody has a right to know about it. What pisses me off is that there are these fuckin' things called "slow news days." On those days, TV freaks out. They have to come up with ways to invent bad news. They tell you about the bad things that might happen.

"Tonight on *Eyewitness News*, the asteroid that might hit Earth."

"Do you feel safe on the train? Well, here are a few things that might happen to you."

They put fear into you. Ever since 9/11, the news has a standard story on slow news days. Here are all the ways that a terrorist might do something horrible. Pisses me off. Not only is it scaring the shit out of people for no particular reason but, just in case the fuckin' terrorist hadn't thought of the clever way to cause mayhem, the fuckin' TV newspeople thought of it for him.

In case the fuckin' terrorist couldn't figure out our vulnerability, the best place to put a fuckin' bomb or whatever, the smiling crew at *Eyewitness News* will show him. Don't they think the terrorists are watching *Eyewitness News*?

The other day, I'm watching the fuckin' news on a fuckin' slow news day and they got this reporter who's showing anyone who tunes in just how easy it is to get access to the fuckin' reservoirs.

The next day, he's showing how easy it is to get access to a plane at the airport. Turns out you don't pretend to be a fuckin' passenger, you pretend to be an airport employee who

This is Two-Gun Tommy Tetrazini, one of the best hit men in the Tommy Funzi Family out of Canarsie. Then someone clocked him over the head with a lead pipe and from that day on he thought he was Hopalong Cassidy. (author's collection)

loads up the cargo. Well, now everyone knows, you fuckin' morons.

Wake up! Wake up, newspeople, the terrorists are watching, too! Write your congressman about this. It should be against the law to show these things. These newspeople are going too fuckin' far now.

It's gotta fuckin' stop. I'm warnin' you people, and remember you heard it from the Big Man, one day something bad is going to happen and when they ask the terrorist who did it—Abdul Muhammad Kahlil or whatever the fuck his name turns out to be—when they fuckin' ask him how he knew the soft spot in our security system, he's gonna say it was fuckin' simple, he saw it on *Eyewitness News.*

Another thing I hate about the fuckin' news on TV and radio these days is that they don't care about giving you the correct information. They only care about the fucking ratings. Sometimes they don't give you any info at all. They just tell you that they're gonna tell you something later on in the fucking show. It's called a tease, and it sucks. They should give you the fuckin' big news right up front. News is a fuckin' public service, and they fuckin' treat it like a fuckin' murder mystery where you don't find out who the fuck did it until the last fuckin' scene. I'm sick.

Another thing, they got to keep you on edge. If they don't scare the fucking shit out of you, you might change the fucking channel and watch something else. God forbid. Here's something that happened just the other day.

I was listening to the fuckin' news on the radio the other day and they kept saying it over and over again: In a few weeks the terrorists are going to attack again. It's gonna be like another fucking 9/11.

They're fucking getting everybody nervous. You can feel the fucking fear in the air. Then they send some twinkie fucking reporter out to interview the common fucking man on the street on how he feels about the upcoming terrorist attack, the terrorist fucking attack that the fucking newspeople made up in the first place.

This reporter is sticking a microphone in people's fucking faces and saying, "What do you think about the fucking terrorists?" You know, they're fucking lucky that they didn't ask me. You know what I'd say?

I'd tell 'em, "Listen: when my number is up, it's up. I ain't gonna live my fucking life in fear. When your number is up, it's up. I ain't got no fuckin' 'go bag.' Where the fuck am I gonna go if the terrorists attack? East fucking Orange? When you gonna go, you gonna go. We all gotta go, people. Maybe you get there before me, maybe I get there before you."

That's what I'd fuckin' tell 'em. Who the fuck wants to hear this fucking bullshit every day? They do enough hollerin' about the fuckin' war in Iraq, they gotta holler about the terrorists, too? Fuckin' bullshit.

Here's a question. Here's a fuckin' question. Let me ask you something: How come there's no fuckin' terrorism in China? Do you know what the fuckin' Chinese would do to these fuckin' terrorist cocksuckers? I'll tell ya. They'd hang 'em up and fuckin' skin 'em. You don't fuck with them fuckin' Chinese. They got a billion guys in their fuckin' army. Send them to Iraq, they'll start skinnin' the fuckin' Iraqi rat bas-

*The news is showing how easy it is to get access to a plane at the airport. Turns out you don't pretend to be a fuckin' passenger, you pretend to be an airport employee who loads up the cargo. Well, now everyone knows, you fuckin' morons.*

tards alive! You put the fuckin' Chinese in charge and there wouldn't be one fuckin' terrorist left in the fuckin' world. They ain't like us. They got no fuckin' mercy. They'd know how to treat the fuckin' terrorists. You burn the cocksuckers alive, and then you burn their families. You burn their mothers. You burn their fathers, their fuckin' kids, you burn 'em all.

That's the way you teach 'em a fuckin' lesson. You gonna be a terrorist, we're gonna kill your whole fucking family, motherfucker. That'll make 'em think twice before they go out the next time and pull a fuckin' suicide bombing.

I'll send you to fuckin' Allah, you prick. That may be okay but you, you are a suicide bomber after all, but you got to know that your fuckin' family is going with you.

I'll tell ya, it burns my fuckin' ass, these newspeople these days.

## To Tell the Truth

Now as I write this, Hill is runnin' for president and she's still gotta deal with the fuckin' specter of her husband, the man who lied. Did he lie about national security? No. Did he lie about political dirty tricks? No. You know what the fuck he lied about. He lied about getting a fucking blow job.

Now, I like Bill Clinton. I want to make that clear for starters. I think he's a hell of a guy. Handsome. Charismatic. All of his fuckin' problems would have been solved if he had just told the fuckin' truth.

When they asked him, "Did you have sex with that woman, Monica Lewinsky?" he should have said, "What the fuck would you do if a twenty-four-year-old intern came into your fuckin' office and wanted to crawl under your fuckin' desk?"

Here's a guy who had every fuckin' thing goin' for him. He was tall, charismatic, everybody fuckin' loved him. He was the most powerful man in the world, the leader of the fuckin' free world. Goes on TV in front of three hundred fuckin' million Americans and he can't fuckin' tell the truth. That's a politician for ya. Why tell the fuckin' truth when a tangled web of lies will get you into a gigantic mess that might end your fuckin' career, right?

He should have said, "What the fuck would you have done if that woman had wiggled her ass in your face and exposed her breasts to you? What the fuck would you do if she wanted to fuckin' smoke your cigar?"

Well, I'll tell you what the Big Man would do. I'd fuckin' go for it, my fuckin' self. The guy is only fuckin' human. So, big fuckin' deal. He made a fuckin' mistake on account of he's a man and he's got fuckin' needs.

But I guess he got the fuck away with it. He stayed president, he got his fuckin' pension. He gets his quarter-million dollars for every fuckin' speech he gives. He gets his $12 million book deal.

And he keeps his fuckin' wife who's workin' her balls— that's right, I said fuckin' balls—who's workin' her fuckin' balls off to get him back into the White House. But still, the guy could have had a fuckin' legacy.

He could have been remembered as a president who kept the peace and was good for the fuckin' economy. But he couldn't look the American people straight in the eye and tell the fuckin' truth. Just like every other fuckin' politician in the fuckin' world.

Let me ask you this. Am I gonna go hear Bill Clinton give a speech? Am I gonna buy his fuckin' book? No, and you know why? Because I can't believe a single word he says or writes. He's a fuckin' politician.

So take the lesson from Bill fuckin' Clinton and the Big Man. The next time something happens in your fuckin' life, tell the fuckin' truth. They're only gonna find out anyway, so there ain't no point in lyin'.

> *He should have said, "What the*
> *fuck would you have done if*
> *that woman had wiggled her ass*
> *in your face and exposed her*
> *breasts to you? What the fuck*
> *would you do if she wanted to*
> *fuckin' smoke your cigar?"*

## The Harsh Gavel of Judge Caracciolo

Now, when I was a kid back in Brooklyn we had the LL train. Elevated. Now they just call it the L train but same thing. It went along Rockaway Parkway, then into the city, and the last stop was 14th Street and Eighth Avenue on the fuckin' West Side.

And I swear, on every fuckin' platform at every fuckin' stop, all the way from Canarsie to Eighth Avenue, they had vending machines. You could get Chiclets, two in a pack for a penny. They had ice cream machines. Soda machines. You name it.

Today, they're all gone. All fuckin' gone. You could check every inch of every platform from Canarsie to the West Side and you ain't gonna find one fuckin' vending machine. And I'll tell you fuckin' why.

It's the laws today. They're too fuckin' lenient. Back in my time, back in the 1950s, God forbid you got caught robbin' a vending machine. Not only would you get a fuckin' nightstick up your ass, but you'd catch the fuckin' beatin' of your life.

After they scraped what was left of you off the subway platform, they would haul your fuckin' ass into a fuckin' courtroom and a judge would give you five fuckin' years in the state penitentiary. Nobody robbed the fuckin' vending machines.

Today, you can get way with fuckin' murder. They should let me be a fuckin' judge today. Face it, I would look great up there sittin' on the bench in my fuckin' black robe, whackin' away with my fuckin' gavel.

I'll show you what I would do to some of these cocksuckers who are breaking the law today. They're used to being treated with leniency, huh? Well, there'd be nothin' lenient about the way I'd fuckin' treat 'em.

You see all those fuckin' drug dealers today who sell the fuckin' drugs on the corner—the ones who are sellin' the drugs to our kids and everything? LIFE! We put 'em on a fuckin' island until they fuckin' rot. On an island somewhere surrounded by fuckin' ocean. You want to escape from the place, you'd better be able to swim a thousand miles or navigate a raft through a fuckin' hurricane. Nobody's ever gonna get out of that fuckin' place.

The trouble is the judges these days. They're fuckin' liberals out there. They're too fuckin' lenient. Don't let me catch you putting fuckin' graffiti on a fuckin' bus or a fuckin' train. Judge Big Man would dish out some fuckin' blue-collar justice. I'd be callin' for order with a big ol' nasty gavel. I'd be harsher than the fuckin' judges over there in Singapore.

I catch your ass taggin' a wall or a van with spray paint or a fuckin' felt-tip pen and you're gonna get a fuckin' hundred lashes and then a year in jail. Think twice before you vandalize something again.

You got people today who'll tell you that graffiti is fuckin' art. Fuck that! You got museums that say that shit. A year or so ago, the fuckin' Brooklyn Museum had a showing of graffiti art. I can't fuckin' stand it. Graffiti ain't fuckin' art. It's fuckin' vandalism, people. Vandalism. A hundred lashes and a year in fuckin' jail if I'm the fuckin' judge.

Back in the fifties, a lot of these fuckin' street punks didn't even make it to the judge. They got their fuckin' asshole busted open by the fuckin' cops and that was fuckin' that. I, the fuckin' jury. Justice was fuckin' served.

Back in them days, a drug dealer couldn't even fuckin' exist in a neighborhood like mine. Them punks knew better than to try and sell drugs on the street corners in fuckin' Canarsie. It would have been like committing fuckin' suicide.

You try to sell drugs in Canasie during the fuckin' fifties and a fuckin' Wise Guy would put you in the fuckin' cemetery. That's the fuckin' way it was back in those days. But everything fuckin' changed—and it changed for the worse.

> *You see all those fuckin' drug dealers today? We put 'em on a fuckin' island until they fuckin' rot.*

## I Don't Sell Tickets to Fuckin' Phonies

You know what pissed me off about the fuckin' world today? Everybody's a fuckin' phony. You got rich guys who are good lookin' and you got rich women who look like Marilyn Monroe in her prime, you can hate their fuckin' guts, but if you were to meet them—and the fuckin' odds are that you never will but if you did—you'd be nice to them. But not the Big Man.

The Big Man will tell you straight out forward. I tell the truth. No matter what. No matter how much fuckin' money you got. No matter how good looking you are. I'll tell you straight to your fuckin' face.

If I don't like you, you are gonna know I don't like you. I don't fuckin' fool around. I come right out with it. Now, I'm in the ticket business, and a lot of guys in the ticket business, I hate their guts. They couldn't buy a ticket off me if they offered me $20 million.

I'd throw the ticket away in the fuckin' garbage first before I sold it to one of them motherfuckers I can't stand. I'd throw it in the fuckin' garbage, and you know why? Because I don't like 'em, that's why!

If I don't like you, you get nothing. The fuckin' ticket goes in the garbage. And nine times out o' fuckin' ten, the reason I don't like a person is because he's a fuckin' phony. There's a shitload of fuckin' phonies today.

These fuckin' phonies, you know what the fuck they do? They let the almighty dollar rule their mind. Not me. I don't fall for no bullshit.

*Now, I'm in the ticket business, and a lot of guys in the ticket business, I hate their guts. They couldn't buy a ticket off me if they offered me $20 million.*

## Three Easy Steps to Taking Over Atlantic City

I was watching the fuckin' *Apprentice* show the other night. You know that show. Fuckin' Donald Trump runs these fuckin' kids through the paces to see who's gonna have the fuckin' honor of being his fuckin' slave.

Well, on this show, he's dividing up the kids into two teams and each team had to come up with promotional ideas to get customers to come into his casinos down there in Atlantic City. I think Trump has got the wrong fuckin' idea.

The show is okay, but if he really wants promotional ideas that are going to put new suckers, er, customers into his casinos, then he should ask a street guy—a street guy like me. You don't ask fuckin' college kids. They don't know their ass from their elbow, these fuckin' kids.

No, you ask a guy like me and I'm gonna tell you how to fuckin' do it. It's very simple. Listen up, Trump. I'm gonna give you three fuckin' ideas right now. These ideas are worth a fuckin' million dollars and I'm gonna give 'em to you for fuckin' free, so pay attention.

First of all, no vig on a crap table. What's the fuckin' vig? That's the house advantage. The house has made up the rules in their favor. The game is rigged. For example, if you bet $5 that, on the next roll of the dice, "snake eyes" (one, one) will appear, you are being played for a sucker. Play that bet for every roll of the dice for an extended period of time and eventually all of the money—which once upon a time had been yours—will be the casino's. Even if snake eyes comes up once for every thirty-six rolls of the dice, as would be expected, you will steadily lose your money because you will win only $150 each time it happens, rather than the $175 you would have to make to break even. Eliminate the vig, Donald Trump. You'll still make a mint because people are fuckin' stupid and they don't know how to bet, and you'll pull in a fuckin' zillion new customers who don't go to your fuckin' craps tables today because they know the game is rigged.

Second idea: all blackjack games should use a single deck of cards. Now, smart guys like Trump, they offer multideck blackjack games, because they think it makes it harder for card-counters to win a fortune. They fear that a guy like that

Dustin Hoffman character in *The Rain Man* is going to come in and break the fuckin' bank. But they got the wrong idea. That guy might exist one in a million, but the average gambler can't fuckin' count cards. He might think he can count cards, and he'll lose his mortgage payment trying, but the guy that can actually do all the fuckin' math in his head while a rapid-fire blackjack game is goin' on, is very rare. You play with one fuckin' deck and now all the players think they can fuckin' count cards, and they think they can win, and they don't realize that they're wrong until their fuckin' chips are gone.

The third idea is, you feed the customers. They will gamble longer hours if they are well fed, so here's what you do. Have the restaurant serve a sixteen-ounce sirloin steak and a baked potato for $4.99. Who the fuck is going to go to any other casino? And it ain't like you're gonna lose fuckin' money. What will it cost you? Three bucks for the food, another buck or two for the labor, and you break even. But you got sixteen thousand fuckin' people standing in line for their meal and every fuckin' one of them is gonna drop a bundle in your casino, especially on a Friday or Saturday night.

You would wipe out the fuckin' competition. You eliminate the vig at the craps table, you play blackjack with a single deck of cards, and you serve steak and potatoes cheap, and, within a fuckin' year, yours will be the only fuckin' casino on the fuckin' boardwalk. Come on, Trump. Let's see what you're made out of.

You take the Big Man's idea and you'll have every high roller from the East Coast to the West Coast comin' to gamble in your casino.

> *You eliminate the vig at the craps table, you play blackjack with a single deck of cards, and you serve steak and potatoes cheap, and, within a fuckin' year, yours will be the only fuckin' casino on the fuckin' boardwalk.*

## Here's How to Lower Gas Prices

I'll tell you what royally pisses off the Big Man today. Fuckin' gas prices. They're fuckin' out of control. I went to the fuckin' gasoline station the other day to fill up my fuckin' car with gas. It cost me sixty-two fuckin' dollars to fill up the fuckin' tank.

Three, four bucks a gallon. Just another sign that the fuckin' world is comin' to an end. I'll tell you what I'd do if I was President Bush.

I'd have fifteen thousand oil tankers every day goin' over there to Iraq. They would pull up to Iraq and say, "Fill 'er up." You know what it's fuckin' costing us to fight that fuckin' war over there every day? A fuckin' bundle, that's what.

I say, we get some of our fuckin' money back. I say fuck 'em. Take the fuckin' oil. Them hippies say that this war has been about oil all along; well, the Big Man says that if it ain't, then it should be.

Let's take the fuckin' oil and lower the fuckin' prices at the fuckin' gas tank back here in the United States. We deserve the oil, not just for all the money we spent over there but for all the soldiers we lost. Every day, we got soldiers getting fuckin' killed over there. You know what I say? It's our fuckin' oil now. What do you think? You think it's their fuckin' oil? Fuck no. It belongs to us. Fuck them.

Them fuckin' oil tycoons can stick it up their ass, chargin' almost five bucks a gallon. I hope you motherfuckers die with every fuckin' dime. Bring the fuckin' prices down so the workin' man can support his family.

And another fuckin' thing, as long as I'm talkin' about the Persian Gulf, how about that fuckin' Kuwait? Are they a bunch of ungrateful bastards or what? Back in 1991, when Iraq invaded Kuwait, we went over there and we saved their asses. Their oil was burnin', the Iraqis were rapin' their fuckin' women; if it wasn't for us, Kuwait would be fuckin' dead. I say, we go in there and take their fuckin' oil, too. You send another few thousand oil tankers over there to fuckin' Kuwait, say, "Fill 'er up," and before long you'd have the price of fuckin' gas down to twenty-five cents a gallon, where it ought to be.

And don't even fuckin' get me started on Saudi Arabia. Fuck them Saudi Arabians! They got enough fuckin' money. I say, we take their fuckin' oil, too. Fill 'er up! Fill 'er the fuck up—right to the fuckin' brim.

You know what the fuck is wrong with people? The more money they got, the more they fuckin' want. They ain't satisfied livin' in a thirty-room palace. They've got to have a fuckin' five-hundred-fuckin'-room palace. They ain't satisfied with three fuckin' Rolls-Royces. They've got to have fucking twenty fuckin' Rolls-Royces.

I mean, come on! How much can you fuckin' eat? How many fuckin' suits can you fuckin' wear? How many fuckin' shoes can you fuckin' wear? Give the fuckin' rest of the world a fuckin' break, you know? There's a lot of fuckin' people out there who deserve fuckin' help. We should help our own people in this fuckin' country. People are starvin' here.

You know it bothers me, this rich gettin' richer and the

poor gettin' poorer bullshit. It fuckin' bothers me. Now, I ain't a fuckin' political guy. But, jeez, elect me fuckin' president and I'll show you what I can fuckin' do. I'd make sure that people who are so fuckin' rich that they couldn't possibly spend all of their fuckin' money would give some of that uncountable wealth back so that a starvin' kid doesn't have to go to bed hungry. That's what the fuck I would do.

And another thing, as long as I'm on a fuckin' roll. We spent trillions and fuckin' trillions of dollars building nuclear weapons, right? We have nuclear weapons up the fuckin' wazoo. We got stockpiles of the fuckin' shit. Well, I got a fuckin' question: When the fuck are we ever gonna use 'em? We gonna use 'em when it's too fuckin' late.

You know what I would do with fuckin' Iraq, if I was president? I'd get the Americans out of there and just set up some cameras. Then I'd have a pay-per-view every month showing Iraqis fuckin' killing each other. Wouldn't cost a dime and might even make a buck or two to feed a hungry poor kid!

> *I'd have fifteen thousand oil tankers every day goin' over there to Iraq. They would pull up to Iraq and say, "Fill 'er up."*

## One Size Does Not Fuckin' Fit All

The Big Man is thinkin' of takin' out a lawsuit against all of these companies that say, "One size fits all." I ordered a robe once on the Internet. The Web site said, "One size fits all." The fuckin' thing showed up, and I couldn't even fuckin' get it over one arm.

I'm a six-X Tall. One size does not fit fuckin' all!

You ever check into a fuckin' hotel and they got the fuckin' robe hangin' in there in the room? The compli-fuckin'-mentary robe. Its label says, "One size fits all." Who the fuck do they design these robes for, fuckin' Chinese midgets?

I think all of us big people, we ought to band together and form a fuckin' class action—a class-fuckin'-action lawsuit. Tell 'em who the fuck are you kiddin' with this one-size-fits-all bullshit?

Power to the big people! Six-X Tall! Six-X Tall! Six-X Tall! Six-X Tall! Six-X Tall! Six-X Tall! Six-X Tall! Six-X Tall!

*I ordered a robe once on the Internet. The Web site said, "One size fits all." The fuckin' thing showed up, and I couldn't even fuckin' get it over one arm. They should've said "one size fits all but me!"*

## How to Solve the Overcrowded Prison Problem

I was thinkin' the other day, imagining myself a judge, Judge Caracciolo, or a big-time fuckin' politician. I was thinkin' of all the things I would do to make the world a fuckin' better place in which to fuckin' live, the ways in which I would serve the good people of America.

The first thing I would do is, I'd take all of the hard-core criminals, the guys on death row, all of the gang members who'd rather slash your fuckin' face than look at you, all of the rapists who give women about as much respect as toilet paper, and I'd ship 'em over there to Afghanistan and Iraq. Give 'em a fuckin' shotgun, enough food for a fuckin' week or so, which is more than they fuckin' deserve, and see how fuckin' tough they are.

We got a problem with overcrowded prisons, overcrowded fuckin' jailhouses. The fuckin' jails and prisons are bustin' at the fuckin' seams. I say empty 'em out and send all of them fuckin' motherfuckers to the war zone.

You know what the problem is. It's all them fuckin' softies out there who believe in rehabili-fuckin'-tation. They don't agree with me. They think that these people can be fixed in fuckin' prison and put back into our society.

Well, let me tell you, I don't want these motherfuckers back in my fuckin' society. I say, put them back in Afghanistan's society. Let's stick 'em in Iraq's society. Believe me, if I was in fuckin' charge, that's what I would fuckin' do.

Those murderers and rapists would all be crying like fuckin' babies. They'd miss their fuckin' cozy prison cell. They'd be out in the fuckin' desert, hidin' in a fuckin' hole. We'd find out how fuckin' tough they are, and we wouldn't have to spend taxpayers' hard-earned money feeding the rat bastards anymore.

> *I don't want these motherfuckers back in my fuckin' society. I say, we put them back in Afghanistan's society.*

# Nathan's Hot Dog Eating Contest

Now, some of you smarter readers might know that the fuckin' hot dog was invented in my home town, right in fuckin' Brooklyn. Coney fuckin' Island. Nathan's hot dogs. Best fuckin' hot dogs on Earth.

Nathan's has been there for a hundred fuckin' years, sellin' their fuckin' wieners, but one thing they got now that they didn't have when I was a kid is the "Hot Dog Eating Contest." That's where these food hounds wolf down as many hot dogs as they can in a short period of time and the one who eats the most hot dogs wins money and a trophy.

They even show the event on TV now. I want to tell you, it's risky business. As long as you keep watching the winner, you're okay—but the second you start lookin' at the losers, you got problems. The rules are that regurgi-fuckin'-tation is a DQ, a disqualification, so you got guys pukin' and tryin' to make it look like they didn't puke. It's fuckin' gross.

Now, even more amazing than the fact that the fuckin' contest exists at all, is the fact that the winner for, like, nine years straight was this skinny Japanese guy who weighed about as much as my fuckin' pinkie. I don't know if this guy had a fuckin' hollow leg or what, but he'd be in there with guys who weighed three times as much as he did, and when they counted up the hot dogs, he was the fuckin' winner.

The little guy revolutionized the fuckin' sport. He was the one who figured out that you've got to eat the hot dog and the bun separately. He was the one who brought a glass of water up there with him and dunked the bun in the water before he ate it.

The other poor bastards were tryin' to get their spit to do all the work, to get the fuckin' bread slippery enough so they could swallow that. But this little Japanese guy figured it out. He dunked.

Now everyone dunks. That's fuckin' progress.

Well, I mention that, because I want to make a challenge. I want to challenge anyone, and I mean anyone, amateurs, professional speed eaters, whatever the fuck you are, to a steak-eating contest.

If I'm gonna make a pig out of myself, I ain't gonna do it over hot dogs. I'm gonna do it for some quality meat. We"ll have the fuckin' contest at Peter Luger's in Brooklyn. We'll see who can eat the most steak in one hour.

If fuckin' ESPN wants to show up with fuckin' cameras, put it on TV, that's okay, too. We could be eatin' prime in prime time. Ten-thousand-dollar cash prize for the man, woman, or child who can eat the most sirloin in an hour.

So, if there's anybody out there who thinks he can eat more steak than the Big Man, you call me up with the challenge and the Big Man will take you on.

> *The winner for, like, nine years straight was this skinny Japanese guy who weighed about as much as my fuckin' pinkie.*

## Back in the Old Days When I Was Happy

You know, readers, I ain't happy no more. I used to be happy, but no fuckin' more. Back when I was a kid, when I was fifteen, sixteen, seventeen, eighteen, yeah, those were the good old days. That was the golden age, let me tell ya.

We used to drive around, smoke a little reefer. We'd smoke it out of a corncob pipe, like we was Popeye or fuckin' General Douglas MacArthur. And we would laugh, laugh, laugh. I'd laugh for fuckin' hours.

We'd turn on the Top Forty radio and every song was fuckin' great. You had the Beatles and the Stones and the Kinks and the fuckin' Who. Every fuckin' song was a classic.

And then we'd get real fuckin' hungry. We'd get starving. And we'd go over to White Castle. I'd order eight fuckin' hamburgers and a large Coke. Cost me ninety-six cents. The whole fuckin' night was cheap.

Gas was cheap. You could cruise the car around for hours and hours and it didn't fuckin' cost you nothin'. The corn-cob pipe cost a quarter. Eatin' was less than a buck. The reefer was a nickel bag and it was big. Shit, if you had pa-pers, you could roll ten fuckin' fat joints for your five bucks.

On the nights when we didn't go to the White Castle, we'd drive down to Coney Island to Nathan's, where the hot dogs were a quarter. Me, I used to get six dogs and two sodas. Cost me less than two dollars.

Then, if you wanted, you could get a big piece of water-melon for a quarter. Big fuckin' piece. Or you could go around to the side of Nathan's, where they sold corn on the cob. That cost a quarter, too. The corn on the cob would be fuckin' drippin' with butter!

A dozen clams! You could get a dozen littleneck clams, seventy-five cents the fuckin' guy would charge you. The guy would cut 'em fresh for you, right there. How's that? Seventy-five fuckin' cents.

And then if we were really in the mood, if we were really fuckin' in the mood, we'd go to fuckin' Junior's over there on Flatbush and DeKalb, right by the fuckin' Paramount Theater. We'd order a big cheeseburger deluxe and the straw-berry cheese pie or the strawberry shortcake.

And in the summertime, when it was hot, the houses didn't have air-conditioning. You had to fuckin' sleep on the roof or on the fire escape just to get a little breeze. Some folks had a fan, but it just blew the hot air around. The cars didn't have no air-conditioning either. You had to roll down the fuckin' window. I don't know if the kids today could put up with that.

We didn't have swimming pools, like the fuckin' kids today do. Back in Canarsie, we used to open up the fire hydrants. Some days, the temperature would be hotter than a fuckin' hundred degrees. We'd open up the fuckin' fire hydrants and the fire department would come around and shut 'em off.

Yeah, back then we had very little, but it didn't fuckin' matter because we were happy. Everything was good. We didn't

Two of the teachers from my elementary school, Miss Biddy on the left and Miss Swackhammer on the right, keeping an eye on us at recess. Don't let the kind faces fool you—these old broads were tougher than the hamsteaks at Kelsey's Saloon. (author's collection)

have no problems because we didn't know no fuckin' better. We didn't know about air-conditioning or swimming pools.

Everyone used to go out to Coney Island on the really hot days, or to Brighton Beach. You'd have to take the hot, hot subway train there. Hard to imagine now. No air-conditioning on the subway, either. They had windows that opened, which let the hot tunnel air in, didn't fuckin' cool things off at all. They had fans that blew the hot air around. The subway smelled different back then, too, especially in the fuckin' summer. You could smell the humanity. That's the way it was back in Brooklyn back in the old days, back in the fuckin' fifties.

We used to go down there to Pat and Judy's pizzeria down there in Canarsie. Over there on 92nd Street. It ain't there no more, God bless 'em. I used to get a whole fuckin' pizza. Pure. None of this shit made in a machine. Fuckin' handmade. Handmade sauce. Real mozzarella. None of this fuckin' plastic shit they put on there today. And it cost a dollar—a dollar for the whole fuckin' pie. Now it's two fuckin' bucks for a fuckin' slice and it's garbage. Then: Meatball sandwich: fifty cents. Veal and peppers: fuckin' sixty-five cents. *Marrrone*, was it fuckin' good! Today, they give you garbage. Burger King. Wendy's. It's fuckin' garbage.

Do you know who eats at the fast-food restaurants these days? Fuckin' people who don't know any better. That's who. Fuckin' morons. They don't know about good fuckin' food.

Back in the old days, I swear, you went into a Chinese restaurant and they had real fuckin' tablecloths. Cloth napkins. You ordered the combinations. One from column A and one from column B. You could get chicken chow mein, fried rice, and an egg roll, and they'd give you a choice of tomato egg drop, chicken egg drop, or wonton soup as an appetizer. Plus, you got fuckin' dessert: pie, ice cream, Jell-O. A dollar and a fuckin' quarter—I swear. I take an oath.

Ahhhh, those were the days.

> *Every song was fuckin' great. You had the Beatles and the Stones and the Kinks and the fuckin' Who.*

## The Big Man Tackles Computer Technology

I'm goin' out of my mind today, folks—I'm goin' out of my fuckin' mind. I been at the computer all fuckin' mornin', trying to learn a new program. I been workin' on a computer now for about six, seven years. I know how to turn it on and off, that's about it. I know how to use a few programs. I know how to go on the Internet and surf around. I can read my e-mail and write back if I want to, but that's it. Everything else that you're supposed to do on the fuckin' computer, well, it's like fuckin' Greek to me.

That's because it's too fuckin' complicated, and even if you do have the patience and the time to learn how to do it, they're comin' out with something fuckin' new every other fuckin' day. It'll drive you fuckin' nuts.

You got to be a fuckin' rocket scientist to keep up with all the fuckin' new computer programs they got comin' out these days. I can't do it, and I ain't alone. Most fuckin' people are in the same boat.

The computer costs you an arm and a leg because you can use it to be an architect and design fuckin' houses with fuckin' solar panels to produce your own energy like the fuckin' space station and you can use it to take apart a car engine and put it back together again, but most fuckin' people just know how to turn it on and off and use the fuckin' Internet.

If I was a fuckin' kid today—twelve, thirteen years old—I'd go to fuckin' computer school. I'd learn to be a computer scientist. Those guys, they made fuckin' billions of dollars and I don't even know what the fuck they do.

They're makin' all that money makin' expensive and complicated programs and then selling them to people who know how to turn the fuckin' computer on and off and that's about it. You could rule the fuckin' world if you knew how to work one of these fuckin' computers, but nobody does. People don't know their ass from their fuckin' elbow, but we're all fuckin' buying computers that are more sophisticated that the ones that put fuckin' man on the moon!

I tell you, I been having a tough day with my computer. All I want to do is learn how to do something that don't have to do with the fuckin' Internet, and I'm gettin' so frustrated I feel like picking up the fucking computer and throwing it out the fucking window.

> *You got to be a fuckin' rocket*
> *scientist to keep up with all the*
> *fuckin' new computer programs*
> *they got comin' out these days.*

## Hey, You Cowardly Protesters, Come to New York!

Now I watch *Fox News* at night on account of I can't stand any of that reality-show crap they got on the networks. I like *The O'Reilly Factor*, but I got a bone to pick with them guys that come on after him, Cannity and Holmes, or Hannity and Colmes, whatever the fuck they are.

The other night, I'm watching the fucking show and this Hannity guy is interviewing a woman whose job it is to go around and disrupt the funerals of soldiers who got killed over there in fuckin' Iraq.

She leads protests and he's interviewing her. Now, he's an educated guy. I figure he's probably a college graduate. He's a newsman. I figure he's got some brains, but then I gotta fuckin' wonder.

I mean, you didn't have to look at this woman for more than a couple of fuckin' seconds to figure out that she's a fuckin' nutjob. I can see it. Everyone watching the fuckin' TV show can see it. She went on a fuckin' journey to the center of her mind and she fuckin' didn't come back.

This woman looks like she had just escaped from the fuckin' nuthouse. How come Hannity can't fuckin' figure it out? He's asking her serious fucking questions. Why the fuck is he even botherin' with her?

The only thing I got to say to these people who are holding protests while the poor soldiers are getting buried, is this: Come to Brooklyn! Come to the Bronx. Come to fuckin' Queens. Come over here and start some fuckin' trouble, you fuckin' fruitcakes. You fuckin' stool-pigeon rat bastards.

Try that shit in my neck of the fuckin' woods and you're the one who'll get carried out of there in a fuckin' box. These

*Come to Brooklyn! Come to the Bronx. Come to fuckin' Queens. Come over here and start some fuckin' trouble, you fuckin' fruitcakes.*

protester whackjobs are smart enough to only do their thing in small towns where they know the fuckin' people are meek.

Come on! You go to fuckin' Harlem. Let's see the size of your nads. Go up there to fuckin' Harlem and start a protest while they're burying one of them brave black soldiers who was killed in Iraq or over there in Afghanistan. See where it fuckin' gets ya. They'll carry you away and all the fuckin' assholes you're with in fuckin' boxes. That'll stop this fuckin' shit. You mark the Big Man's words. One day, these protesting motherfuckers are gonna run into an irate guy and he's gonna kill a handful of them cocksuckers.

Come to New York, you fuckin' cowards!


## Imagine if Condoms Came in Sizes

You know, I know a lot of guys out there are a little bit shy, a little bit bashful, when they go into their local drugstore and ask for a condom. I know, because I've felt that way myself. I admit it.

Could you imagine if they came in fuckin' sizes? Extra-small, small, medium. Maybe they wouldn't call it extra-small. They'd call it fuckin' "cadet." Imagine goin' into the fuckin' pharmacy and asking for a pack of Trojans. The guy says, "What size?" And you've got to say, "Cadet."

The guy would say at the top of his lungs, "Hey, Joe, we got any cadet condoms back there behind the fuckin' counter?"

There'd be large sizes, too. Large, double-large. Triple X. Quad-fuckin'-druple X. No, they wouldn't call it quadruple X. They'd call it "Magnum."

*They wouldn't call it extra-small. They'd call it fuckin' "cadet."*

## I Ain't Nothin' If I Ain't Tolerant

Now, the Big Man is a tolerant guy. I get pissed off at a lot of shit and I want everyone to speak English and I want to see the fuckin' terrorists boiled in oil, but that don't mean I think everyone's got to be just like me.

I grew up in Brooklyn. The fucking melting pot. There were all kinds of different fuckin' people all living together and all riding in the same subway cars, and you learned that you got to all get along.

That goes for people from different countries. People with fuckin' different religions, and it goes for fuckin' gay people, too. I remember a few years back there was all kinds of fuckin' fuss when that movie came out, *Backdoor Mountin* or whatever the fuck it was. It was a fuckin' gay cowboy movie. Not my cup of fuckin' tea but what the fuck, I say.

I said at the time and I'll say it now, if you don't want to see two cowboys kissing, then just don't go to the fuckin' movie. People got to learn to mind their own fucking business in this fucking world.

I got nothin' against the fuckin' gay people. Why should I? Why should you? Mind your own fuckin' business. As long as the fuckin' gay people ain't botherin' you, what the fuck do you care who they're schtuppin'?

Ain't you got bigger problems? Ain't you got your own life

to worry about? The biggest problem on your fuckin' plate is that they're makin' fuckin' gay movies? You must be pretty lucky if that's your biggest worry.

It don't concern you. Who gives a fuck? Fuck it. It's like these cocksuckers who go out on a highway. There's a fuckin' accident on the other side. They slow down so that they're movin' like fuckin' snails so they can see everything there is to see. Rubberneckin', it's called—and they're holdin' up all the traffic behind them so everyone is fuckin' late gettin' home.

*As long as the fuckin' gay people ain't botherin' you, what the fuck do you care?*

Everybody's got to sit in fuckin' traffic for a fuckin' hour. Keep movin'. Fucking go, you cocksucker. It ain't none of your business. You can't do nothin' about that fuckin' accident. Keep goin'. People are nosy bastards, that's what it boils down to.

Anyway, let the gay people live any fuckin' way they want to. It ain't got nothin' to do with you and it ain't none of your fuckin' business. They ain't botherin' nobody. If you don't want to be around them, then don't be around them! Give them people a fuckin' break. If you don't like gay movies, then don't go but leave 'em alone, for Chrissakes.

## The Guys Who Really Have Balls

You know, the Big Man is a little bit older now and I've started thinkin' about things, things I didn't used to think about. Back in the old days, we all thought we were fuckin' tough guys. We used to fight with our fists in the schoolyard. We didn't use no weapons. There were no fuckin' guns. No knives. Nobody brought a fuckin' baseball bat to the fuckin' party.

We thought we were tough guys. But lately it dawned on me, you know who the tough guys are? The tough guys are them firefighters. They run into the burning building everyone else is running out of. And they have to do it every fuckin' day.

The cops are tough guys, too. Do you know what it is to be a cop today? You've got to go out there into the streets and deal with the criminal element that's out there today, All them fuckin' drug dealers and rat bastard criminals. They've all got guns, knives. You know, they'll shoot a cop in a minute.

I'll tell you who else are tough guys. All them brave young soldiers. Tough as fuckin' nails. I mean, you got eighteen-nineteen-year-old kids goin' over there to Iraq and Afghanistan and fighting on the front lines.

Those are the fuckin' tough guys, in my book. Those are the guys with fuckin' balls. You know what I'm sayin'? Forget about these other fuckin' people. Take it from the Big Man, these guys—these firemen and cops and soldiers—they got balls and they got 'em every day of the week, three hundred and fuckin' sixty-five days a year.

*The tough guys are them firefighters. They run into the burning building everyone else is running out of. And they have to do it every fuckin' day.*

## Tragic Misers and Melt-in-Your-Mouth Prosciutt'

Generous people, I like. It's the cheap bastards I can't stand. As I write this, I have fallen off my diet big fuckin' time, but I'm lovin' it. Some people in this world are generous and sometimes they're generous with food and I just got to take advantage.

One of those generous people is my little friend TJ. Not to mention Joey and Tommy. They brought me over some fresh prosciutt'. Fresh mozzarell'. Five, six loaves of fresh Italian bread. *Marrone a mia!* That prosciutt' melted in my mouth. Every fuckin' thing they gave me was fuckin' delicious. They are a bunch of sports, I'll tell ya. They really want to put me into the hospital with all this food.

Ahhhh, but I'm happy. If everybody was as generous as TJ and Joey and Tommy, I'd be a happy fuck, but they ain't.

The world's filled with cheap bastards. And you don't have to be a self-important publicity hog like Donald Trump to be a cheap bastard, either. Even the everyday man, the working Joe, can be a cheap bastard.

It's all a fuckin' matter of attitude.

All over the country, in every economic bracket, you got these fuckin' people who spend every fuckin' minute of the fuckin' day worrying about a fuckin' dollar. That's all that's on their minds.

These are the type of people that, when they get a check in the mail—even if it's only for a few fuckin' dollars, their five-fuckin'-dollar rebate from buying electronic equipment on sale—they can't wait to get dressed to get to the fuckin' bank so they can fuckin' deposit it. They got only one leg inside their pants when they go runnin' out of the house, waving the check in the air, headin' down to the fuckin' bank on the corner so they can fuckin' deposit that thing.

You know the fuckin' type. If you told them they had to wait a day or two before putting the fuckin' check in the fuckin' bank, they'd act like you asked them to hold their fuckin' breath for that long. Every fuckin' night, they go by themselves to the corner so they can look at their bankbook, count their fuckin' money.

"How much do I have today? Oooh, fuckin' twenty-seven cents more than yesterday."

Fuck that shit!

Those people count their fuckin' money and they start to pant and swoon and it's like they're fuckin' havin' sex when they count their fuckin' money. That's the way they fuckin' get their fuckin' rocks off.

These are the same people that wouldn't fuckin' buy themselves a can of fuckin' sardines even if they were starvin', because they don't want to spend the fuckin' money. They got empty pockets.

These people must fuckin' keep all of their money in the bank. I sure as hell know they never got any fuckin' money on them. You could go out to eat with them every week for three fuckin' years and every time the fuckin' check came, it would be the same fuckin' story. They ain't got no fuckin' money on them.

"Sorry, I must have left my wallet at home."

Go fuck yourself, you fuckin' cheap bastard. That's what the fuck I say. You say you've got no fuckin' money on you. You never got no money on you. You're too fuckin' cheap! You spend all of your fuckin' time in the fuckin' bank because you got to know how much money you got every day right down to the last fuckin' cent, but you can't even carry a couple bucks in your back fuckin' pocket for when you go to a restaurant to eat? Fuck you.

And do you know what fuckin' happens to these fuckin' cheap bastards? As sure as shit, they end up dying! Dying with every dime! They spent so much time counting their money that they never got around to spending any of it, and that's the fuckin' fun part. They spent so much time counting their fuckin' money that they never got to enjoy their fuckin' life. It's sad.

Luckily for me and the rest of the world TJ, Tommy, and Joey are not like that. They let it go! They got it and they're spreadin' it around, and the Big Man says thank you, thank you, thank you! They're not afraid. They're loose with a buck. I'm sick of these fuckin' misers out there. They spend all of their time in the fuckin' bank and they end up dead.

So let that be a lesson to you from the Big Man: Get out there, get out the fuckin' door, and spread around that money!

> *Those people, it's like they're fuckin' havin' sex when they count their fuckin' money. That's the way they fuckin' get their fuckin' rocks off.*

## Make a Reality Show That's Really Real and Maybe I'll Watch

In my first book, *Go F\*\*\* Yourself*, I told you all about how much I hate reality shows. I explained that I couldn't even watch a reality show all the way through. I always got fuckin' embarrassed for those fucking people.

These contestants, they will do anything to make money. They don't care how much you fuckin' humiliate them, they stay eager, as long as there might be a buck in it or a flash of fame for them down the fucking line.

The other thing I can't fuckin' stand about reality shows is that there ain't no reality about them. They take faded people from the fringes of show business, has-fuckin'-beens, and never-fuckin'-weres, and they put 'em in a house to see what happens.

What the fuck is real about that? So I had an idea the other day. What if they made a reality show that really was real. What if they took a regular guy, a guy making $100,000 a year, not a bum, not a millionaire, and they put this guy in New York City. They put the cameras on him and they say, "Go ahead. Survive."

They always spend a billion dollars taking these survivor type shows to China or some island in the south Pacific or something like that. Why don't they save a buck or two and just drop all of their contestants in a New York City crack-house? I wouldn't watch it, but I'll bet they'd get good ratings—and imagine how much they could cut down on the fuckin' production costs. Better yet, take the fuckin' contestants and put them in one of them New York City sweatshops where they can work next to the illegal aliens for sixteen fuckin' hours a day, makin' two fuckin' dollars an hour. Even better than that, let's take the fuckin' contestants and throw them into the fuckin' Atlantic Avenue Armory, where they got the fuckin' homeless shelter. The fuckin' place looks like Dracula's fuckin' castle and it's filled with real-life vampires. First contestant out alive wins the fuckin' show. Those people they might be able to cook their own rodents in a Burmese jungle but put 'em in a homeless shelter in Brooklyn, and they'll all fuckin' quit in two hours. Put some cameras in there and watch the fun. That's fuckin' reality.

Here's where it's all headed. Mark my fuckin' words. There used to be three fuckin' networks. Now there's about five fuckin' hundred of them. Every fuckin' TV executive is getting desperate for ratings. And it shows.

It's only a matter of time before there are reality shows where people really die. I'll give you a fuckin' reality show. There'll be a new game show on channel 516. Russian Roulette.

You get a fuckin' six-shooter. You put one fuckin' bullet in the chamber. You spin the chamber and then you say your fuckin' prayers. The announcer'll say shit like, "Johnny will pull the trigger . . . after these announcements."

Win and you get the fuckin' million dollars. Lose and you get your fuckin' brains blown out on national TV. The next day, all the news shows will show your messy demise again and fuckin' again, sometimes in super-slow motion so we can see your splattering fuckin' brains. You mark my words.

There's gonna come a time when shit like that is on TV.

*It's only a matter of time before they got reality shows where people really die.*

## Gay Marriage

I was readin' in the newspaper the other day about this here gay marriage. Look, I want you to know right now, I got nothing against gay people. I don't give a fuck who schtupps who. As far as I'm concerned, let 'em get married. Let 'em all get married and suffer with the rest of us.

That's right. Let 'em suffer. Let 'em go through the divorce and the alimony. You know they're gonna adopt children, so let 'em go through the child support. Why should they get off so fuckin' easy?

What I don't like are these fuckin' people who are anti-gay. What the fuck do they think they are going to do? Do they think they are going to wipe fuckin' gay people off the face of the earth? Are they proposing fucking genocide?

The whole fuckin' country is in an uproar over this gay marriage shit. We got a fuckin' war in Iraq. We got gas prices goin' through the roof, and everyone's upset about what? A couple of queens from Queens want to go in a church and get married by another fuckin' queen?

Leave it alone, people. It don't concern you. People say, "Well, it just doesn't fit the definition of marriage as I understand it." Well, fuck you. Who the fuck gave you the power to tell other people what the fuck to do?

The way I see it, it's just another sign that the world's comin' to an end. We got wars goin' on and people are worried about two happy people who want to get married. Fuck it. Leave 'em the fuck alone.

Some people are gay. There's always been gay people. There's always fuckin' going to be gay people. You can't change them. If a guy doesn't like pussy, you're not going to teach him to like pussy.

You're not going to fuckin' change them. They are here to stay. So you got to fuckin' go along with it. You got to let them do what the fuck they want to do. Let them pursue fuckin' happiness like the rest of us.

As long as they don't interfere with my life, I could give two fucks what they do.

*I don't give a fuck who schtupps who.*

## How Come White-Collar Criminals Don't Get Punished?

I get steamed up every fuckin' night, readin' the newspapers and watching the fuckin' TV news. You know what pisses me off. Fuckin' white-collar criminals. How about them Enron assholes. What about that Michael Bilkin from a few years back?

They steal a fuckin' billion dollars, and they don't do no fuckin' time. That Bilkin guy bilked a fuckin' billion and he got two fuckin' years in Club Fed. That's nothin'. Two fuckin' years. That ain't a fuckin' prison. They go swimmin' every day. They play fuckin' tennis. They shoot fuckin' pool. That eat fuckin' gourmet meals.

What the fuck is goin' on here? Who are these fuckin' judges who sentence these fuckin' guys? Let me be a judge the next time they got one of those white-collar assholes on trial for stealing a billion dollars. Let me sentence one of these rat bastards.

I'd give 'em twenty fuckin' years. Hard time. Down south on one of them fuckin' chain gangs. I'd have 'em diggin' fuckin' ditches, sweatin' their fuckin' balls off. Every fuckin' day. That's what they fuckin' deserve, these rat bastards.

> *Let me be a judge the next time they got one of those white-collar assholes on trial for stealing a billion dollars. Let me sentence one of these rat bastards.*

# Today's Special at the Indian Restaurant: Cat in the Hat

You know, growin' up in Brooklyn, back when I was a kid, you had your Italian restaurants, Chinese restaurants. You had the Jewish deli, you get a nice thick corned beef, pastrami. Turkey club with Russian. Fresh. Real good. They had diners. Steakhouses. And cafeterias.

Today, it's the fuckin' end of the world. You know what kind of food they got out there today? Here's the kind of restaurants they got out there today. They got fuckin' Lebanese, Malaysian, Middle Eastern, Moroccan, South African, Spanish, Southeast Asian, Puerto Rican, Polish, Russian, Romanian, Indian, Turkish, French, German, Tibetan, Ukrainian, Vietnamese, et cetera, et fuckin' cetera.

First of all, you got it from the Big Man straight: I wouldn't fuckin' eat in a fuckin' Indian restaurant if you cut my fuckin' right arm off. You ever walk into one of them Indian joints? The fuckin' stink alone'll kill ya. You walk into an Indian restaurant, it smells like two dead mules. And that shit gets in your clothes. You walk into a fuckin' Indian restaurant for two minutes and you got that smell, that dead-mule smell, in your fuckin' clothes for the rest of the day.

Turkish? Who the fuck can eat Turkish? What do fuckin' Turks eat? They probably eat fuckin' shit! Horse shit is the main course. For dessert, a lovely goose shit.

Vietnamese? That's another fuckin' story. When we were over there in Vietnam, they took fuckin' dogs and cats like fuckin' nothin' and they'd throw that in the fuckin' food.

Middle Eastern? What the fuck are you gonna go eat Middle Eastern for? Those fuckin' people don't even know what a fuckin' bag of beans tastes like. You gonna eat that Middle Eastern shit?

Anyway, folks, it bugs me. All these different types of restaurants and they're all shit. Fuckin' garbage. I say, bring back the good old days. Italian, Chinese, deli, steakhouse, diner, cafeterias. That's all the fuck you need. Good clean fresh food.

*What do fuckin' Turks eat?*
*They probably eat fuckin' shit!*

## How to Wipe Out Convenience Store Shoplifting

The Big Man went into a convenience store the other day to get a cup o' coffee. I've got to lay off the sugar, you know, on account of my weight, so I was looking for Equal. Some folks like Sweet 'N Low. I like Equal. Same shit.

I looked all over for it. Couldn't find it. Up this aisle. Down that. Finally, I said to the guy behind the counter, "Hey, where's the Equal?"

He said, "It's behind the counter here. How many you need?"

I said, "Give me four. How come you keep 'em back there?"

"I got to," he said. "Or people come in here and they steal 'em. The women, they stuff their pocketbooks. Guys, they stuff their pockets. They take all the Equals and all the Sweet 'N Lows and all the sugars. They take all the napkins."

I said to him, "You got video surveillance in here?"

He said, "Yeah."

I said, "Look, whoever gets caught taking the sugar and the

Sweet'N Low, stealin' the fuckin' napkins, take the video and put it up on the fuckin' Internet. And then put it on the fuckin' TV right here in your fuckin' store. You put a big fuckin' graphic up there, says, 'Caught shoplifting.' That'll get rid of these cheap bastards."

Can you imagine the fuckin' balls, goin' into a fuckin' convenience store, stealin' a couple of packs of Sweet'N Lows, sugars, and fuckin' napkins? They got to be a fuckin' miser! A fuckin' miser! They deserve to get put on the fuckin' Internet, the cheap cocksuckers!

I'd put a fuckin' TV in the front window of the fuckin' store and I'd play that fuckin' tape all fuckin' day. Cheap rat bastards. That's the way to get rid of them cocksuckers: embarrass the penny-pinchin' motherfuckers.

> *Whoever gets caught taking the sugar and the Sweet'N Low, stealin' the fuckin' napkins, take the video and put it up on the fuckin' Internet.*

## The Departed Salami (with Apologies to William Monahan)

In my head I could hear the bloozy guitar riffs of the Rolling Scones' classic "Gimme Shellfish." This ain't today's Big Man you see walkin' alone along Canarsie Pier, lost in his thoughts. This is the young, savage Big Man, a man of hunger without end, amen.

I was no one to fuck with back then. Dance with me and you were spittin' teeth, a pas de deux that gave hoods all the way to Brownsville a smile like the fuckin' South Bronx, circa 1976, mostly vacant.

I was gazing out over Jamaica Bay. It looked like the caramel run off of a fleshy flan. I was a younger man, yes. But even then I was a fuckin' man of wisdom. Dig this speech. No, I ain't talkin' to myself. It's a fuckin' voiceover, you putrid Pop-Tart!

"When I was your age, I used to say, you can become food cops or food criminals. Truth is, when you're facing the fuckin' business end of a rock-hard salami, what's the fuckin' difference?"

I had a decision to make. I knew there was a rat in the food cops. I could use subterfuge to dig him out or I could grab my own salami and use it to beat the answer out. I was never a subtle guy. I left the pier—and grabbed my salami.

The food criminals in fuckin' Canarsie are run with a heavy appetite by the Irish mob boss, Frank Limejello. But don't let the fuckin' name fool ya. There was nothin' green about him. Between Limejello and the Big Man, you'd think our motto was "ZPG." That's "zero population growth." It was hard growing up in Canarsie without betraying either Limejello or myself, and, if you did, you joined what the Chinks called the *mou gaan dou*: the fuckin' departed.

The reason I knew Limejello had a rat in my squad was, tit for fuckin' tat, I had a rat in his, Stewy Mulligan. Mulligan had infiltrated Limejello's mob and had earned the trust of the fuckin' big guy himself.

But before Mulligan could make that final leap, up to recipe capo, the leap that would bring down the whole fuckin' soufflé, I had to clean my own fuckin' house. The first guy I wanted to talk to was my favorite stoolie, Squints Calamari. If there was word on the street, he fuckin' knew it; and if he knew it, he'd spill it—for a fuckin' price.

"Look, there's a rat in the food cops and I want this rat.

You understand me? If you tell me who the rat is, there's fifty fuckin' salamis in it for ya."

One thing I learned in life: salami talks.

"Fifty salamis!" His squinty eyes got as big as a pair of buttermilk flapjacks.

"You think you can wrap a johnson like this?" I asked, holding my sausage aloft.

"Johnson?" he said. "Johnson? Who the fuck was that? The president after Kennedy?"

"Fuck you, pudding scum. I gotta hit the rocky road. I gotta meeting."

Calamari hit the streets with salami signs in his eyes. I headed for Greenwood Cemetery to meet a guy, a guy named Rabbi Ribeye. I had an associate come, too, but at a distance. His name was Sammy Semolina, the crustiest motherfucker in all of Brooklyn—at least since Zack Wheat roamed the highly caloric pastures of Ebbets Field. If anything went wrong during the meeting, Semolina's instructions were clear: put two bread sticks right behind his ear.

I entered the marble orchard on the fuckin' Fourth Avenue side. Rabbi Ribeye was right on time. The rabbi was a man of few words and a demented laugh. He was like the cat who just ate the fuckin' canary—that is, if the fuckin' canary was a two-story-high pastrami sandwich on dark rye.

"I like meeting in cemeteries," I said. "It reminds me of where I'm gonna end up." The rabbi laughed. "Look, I need to get that rat. Tell your son. I need to get him. I heard he can bait a trap like no one else."

The rabbi grinned a horrible grin. "Limburger," he said.

"Your son works internal affairs, that right?" I said.

Rabbi Ribeye grunted. I had an envelope in my hand and he couldn't take his eyes off it.

I gave him the envelope. "There's fifty thousand fuckin' food stamps in there."

"That's some gelt," Rabbi Ribeye said. "With this kind of gelt, you'll get your man." Then came the demented laugh again.

"If you're good, I'll get you some fuckin' kosher salami," I added. "A fuckin' bonus."

"I never say no to that," Ribeye said. I looked off to one side and saw Semolina duck behind the tomb of Betty Crocker, two bread sticks in his hand.

"Put the stamps in your pocket," I said to the rabbi. "And don't fuckin' forget who gave 'em to ya."

The scheme bore fruit. Rabbi Ribeye's son came up with a name, and Semolina picked him up outside Junior's. His name was Sgt. Bud "Hops" Barley. Hops had been on the force for about five years and I gotta admit, I never fuckin' liked the guy.

**Grady Fleck, who owned Fleck's Bar and Grille in Canarsie, once threw a "come as a Mexican" night at his joint. Things got a little out of hand. (author's collection)**

He was a little too effervescent, if you catch my fuckin' drift. He'd been off the food beat for the past few weeks. Disa-fuckin'-bility.

I had Barley thrown into a small room at the station, the one that had the egg cartons stapled to the walls.

I turned to Semolina. "You search him?"

Semolina nodded, a little light in his eyes. I thought he was gonna sniff his fuckin' fingers. I told him to get the fuck out of there. Barley and I wanted to be alone. I came armed. In my right hand was the biggest fuckin' salami east of Bensonhurst.

Barley had his left arm in a cast. One corner of my mouth turned up when I saw that plaster. I didn't waste any fuckin' time. I started in the second Semolina shut the door behind him.

"You workin' for Limejello?" I said. Beads of fuckin' sweat pearled his forehead.

"No!" he said. I could see the terror in his eyes. I swung the salami with all my might. The first blow cracked the cast. His screams might have been unpleasant to some. Not me. It was like music. I dig the blooz. I smacked him again until the cast fell off and I was hitting the exposed arm, skinnier than the other because of the atrophied muscles.

"You steal my salami?"

"No!"

Chunks of meat were coming off my weapon now, flying around the room like deli shrapnel. I could hear my voice loud, higher in pitch, hysterical. I was ecstatic, juiced by the crumb-bum's pain.

"You rat bastard, you rat bastard, you rat bastard," I heard. It was like an out-of-fucking-body experience. I kept swinging until my fuckin' arm got tired. Then the door opened and Semolina rushed in, afraid I was killing the motherfucker.

"He's all right. He's all right," I said. Barley was whimpering now, as much in despair as in pain. I threw him a towel. "Here, you rat bastard. Fix yourself up. Get yourself in fuckin' shape. This meeting's adjourned."

With that, I left the room, leaving someone else to clean up the fucking mess. I was feeling fuckin' horny from all that action so I went back to my office and made a quick call. Her name was Tammy Taco, a hot tamale if ever there was one.

In five minutes she was there and the door was locked. I grabbed her ample melons and dove for her pomegranate delta. I had a finger in the pie and an apple in my eye. You couldn't fuckin' see my face but you knew I was smilin'!

She jammed and I jellied and then we danced the "Hava Nagila" dance. Hava neranena, hava neranena! Things were good then.

> *"You think you can wrap a johnson like this?" I asked, holding my sausage aloft.*

## Men Across the Nation Tryin' to Watch Football

Here in the United States of America, every Sunday during the fall, millions and millions of men like myself like to sit in an easy chair, crack open a frosty brew, and watch three or four pro football games.

It's an American tradition! And all would be right with the world except for one thing: Our wives or our girlfriends won't leave us alone. They come right into the room where we're watching the game.

And do they stand off to the side of the TV? No. They got to stand right in front of the fuckin' screen. You can hear the announcer going apeshit—"greatest fucking catch ever!"— and a woman is giving you some fucking bullshit.

"Would you want to go over to CVS? It's double coupons today. My mother wants to know if we can pick her up on the way over. Hey? Hey! I'll bet you didn't hear one word I said."

"I heard every fuckin' word you said! Get your fuckin' ass out from in front of the TV set, someone's scorin' a fuckin' touchdown. Get the fuck away from the TV screen and leave me the fuck alone."

"You don't love me!" she cries. "You just love that stupid football."

Well, I'm gonna tell you, fellas: it goes on every week, in households across this great fucking nation of ours. You want to get even with these women? Here's what you do. The next time your wife or your girlfriend are getting dressed, doin' her makeup, puttin' her hair together, you get on her ass.

"Hey, honey, how would you like to go out shoppin' with me? I've got to go get some meat at Frank the Butcher."

"Can't you see I'm doin' my hair?" she'll whine.

Get right in front of their ass. Show women how it feels to be bothered! Show 'em how it feels! Maybe then they'll leave us the fuck alone when we're watching the game. (But don't piss 'em off too much. Halftime is twelve minutes long. Plenty of time for sex!)

*They got to stand right in front of the fuckin' screen. You can hear the announcer going apeshit—"greatest fucking catch ever!"—and a woman is giving you some fucking bullshit.*

## The Gruesome Twosome

What if the president of a major corporation had a 28 percent approval rating from the stockholders? Say the vice president of this major corporation had an 11 percent approval rating. How long do you think they would stay president and vice president? About two seconds, that's how long. The stockholders would kick those two losers out on their asses.

Well, that's the situation we got in that White House. We got the Gruesome Twosome. Bush/Cheney. Cheney has a fuckin' 11 percent approval rating. Come on, gimme a break. That means nine out of ten Americans think he's doin' a shitass job. Who the fuck is the one that approves? Some pinhead living in a fuckin' freight car?

How the fuck does Cheney get up in the morning and go to work? How can he look himself in the mirror? The whole Bush administration is all fucked up. You know me. I'm not a Republican. I'm not a Democrat. I'm an independent type of guy and I got fuckin' common sense. In seven years, the Gruesome Twosome fuckin' destroyed this country.

Do you know how bad it is out there? Americans are investing in foreign currency. Americans are buying Chinese currency instead of holding the American dollar. That'll give you an idea of just how far down the fuckin' toilet we are.

*I'm thinkin' of learnin' Chinese. China is going to be the number one industrial country in ten years. China will be on top.*

Forget about the war in Iraq. That's another story. The American dollar ain't worth shit.

Me, I'm thinkin' of learnin' Chinese. China is going to be the number one industrial country in ten years. China will be on top. I'll get a head start and learn the language now. "Ohhhh, tinoga, ooowaaa, fuku, fuku two time." Why not? All you readers, you better start learning Chinese.


## How Come Health Food Stores Smell Like Shit?

On a recent Saturday morning, I was lying on my bed snoozing away and the telephone rang. I answered it.

"Hello, can I help you?" I said.

"Yes, do you sell organic chop meat?"

"You got the wrong number, pal."

I dozed off again. Five minutes later, phone rang again. Same thing.

"Hello, can I help you?" I said.

"Yes, do you sell organic chop meat?"

"This is a ticket office. I don't sell no chop meat."

He said, "Isn't this Holistic Foods?"

I said, "You got the wrong number."

A half hour later it happened again, and by this time I was fuckin' furious. What the fuck is organic chop meat? So I dug out the fuckin' phone book and I looked up Holistic Foods. I gave 'em a call and I got the butcher on the line.

"What exactly is organic chop meat?" I asked.

He said, "Well, the cattle, they have a private grazing area. They're hand fed. No drugs, no antibiotics have been injected into their bodies."

I said, "How the fuck do I know that? Is it a written guarantee?"

He said, "I can't tell you that, sir. It comes here straight from the meat-packing department."

So I think this whole organic business is a scam. They want people to think it's healthier but it's the same old shit. Maybe worse. You ever go into a health food store? Goddamn, the stench! You can't even breathe in there. As soon as you open the fuckin' front door, you know you're in the wrong joint. You feel like running out of the place before that stink gets into your clothes.

You ever see some of the people who shop in health food stores? Do they look healthy? Fuck, no. Their fuckin' skin is the color of a pair of old sweatpants and it's hanging off the bone. Those people are fuckin' malnourished, I'm tellin' ya. They look like they've got one foot in the fuckin' grave.

Hey, you con men out there selling this organic shit? Stick it up your fuckin' ass.

*This whole organic business is a scam. They want people to think it's healthier but it's the same old horseshit. Maybe worse.*

## The Stupidest Idea I Ever Heard

The fuckin' world has got no shortage of stupid ideas, so pickin' the stupidest is a tough one. But I think I got it. Hey, remember back when New York State governor Eliot Spitzer wanted to give illegal immigrants driver's licenses? I should stop right there. What the fuck more is there to say? That had to be the fuckin' stupidest fuckin' idea I've ever heard. We should call this guy Pinhead Spitzer.

You'd have thought that the idea would have lasted only until the laughter died down, but the debate went on for fuckin' months before he realized he was the only one on Earth who thought it was a good idea.

Gimme a break. While you're at it, why don't you give 'em free cars, free gasoline coupons, free housing, free health care. Give 'em every fuckin' thing for nothin'. Why the fuck not? Let the fuckin' taxpayer pay the bill.

This Spitzer, he used to be the attorney general. He was a fuckin' crime fighter. What the fuck happened? All of a sudden he shifted fuckin' gears. He thought givin' the illegals driver's licenses would bring 'em out of the fuckin' shadows.

Here's a message for Spitzer. You want to take care of the illegal immigrant problem, send 'em the fuck back where they came from. The last time I heard, this was the United States of America and we've got borders. You've got to pay your dues to get into this fuckin' country. You've got to pay your dues to become a fuckin' citizen.

*This Spitzer, he used to be the attorney general. He was a fuckin' crime fighter. What the fuck happened?*

## The First Time I Ever Saw a Pair of Naked Titties

Ahhhh, I remember growing up in Brooklyn. I was about ten or eleven years old the first time I ever saw a pair of naked titties. Just like fuckin' Campbell's Soup. Mmmm, mmmmm, good.

I went over to my friend's house. He wasn't home. His older sister was home. She was seventeen. She told me to sit down in his room and wait for him. She said she had to go and get dressed.

She went down the hall and I heard the door shut behind her. I waited for a few minutes and then I crept down the hall and peeked through the keyhole. There she was and there they were. Her big titties.

I couldn't believe I was really lookin' at naked titties. I got so goddamn excited. Hey, fellas, you remember that, don'tcha? You remember the first time you saw naked titties?

Speaking of tits, you ever see the size of the tits on Dog the Bounty Hunter's wife? Holy fuckin' shit. Maybe Honey Don't, but I'm thinkin' Honeydew! Heh-heh-heh. What's her name? Beth? She got some pair of fuckin' tits. They're fuckin' HUGE.

She's got enough tits for two men—plus! There ain't a fuckin' man alive that can get them tits in his mouth. Can you imagine the size of her fuckin' nipples? You might get a few licks in, fellas, but you ain't getting them titties in your mouth.

Baaa-ah-ah-ah-loons! What a pair of fuckin' dogs.

Those fuckin' titties need a fuckin' custom-made harness. I don't think there's a department store in the world that she can go in and buy a bra off the rack. Maybe she gets her fuckin' bras from the air force, two parachutes sewn together or some shit.

Anyway, if they cancel the Dog's show on A&E, what the fuck is he worried about? There ain't a men's magazine in the fuckin' world that wouldn't spend three million, four million dollars for pictures of his wife with her humongo tits out.

He's sittin' on a fuckin' gold mine. What man wouldn't buy a magazine that had pictures of Beth's tits in it? I admit it. I'd like to sneak a peek myself—and I would have to fuckin' get down on my knees and peek through a fuckin' keyhole.

And truth is, Dog the fuckin' Bounty Hunter may need to rely on his wife's tits before long. His career prospects as I write this ain't lookin' too sweet. Did you ever hear the expression, "I just got fucked"? Or "I'm fucked"?

Well, that's the situation Dog is in. He's been fucked so hard he may never be able to fuckin' walk again. Duane, you ain't gettin' out of this one. You ain't no fuckin' Houdini. There's no way you're skatin' away from this one alive.

Now, I believe in fuckin' freedom of speech and I think in a free fuckin' world you should be able to use whatever fuckin' word you want. Growin' up in Brooklyn, there was a bad word that meant you, no matter who the fuck you were.

Nigger, kike, greaseball, wop, what the fuck ever. But Dog should have known better. He was havin' what he thought was a private conversation with his son, but his son taped the fuckin' conversation and sold it to the *National Enquirer*.

Nice fuckin' kid, right? Well, Dog should have known that his kid was a mercenary rat bastard and he shouldn't have said nothin' that could be taped and used against him. It hurts to get fucked like that, but the pain must be extra excruciating when your son is the one fucking you, fucking you right out of a profitable TV career. That's what the expression "getting fucked" means. And Dog got fucked by his own fuckin' flesh and blood. There ain't nothin' that hurts more than getting fucked by your own flesh and blood.

Let's face it, folks. Let's face the facts. If they tape-recorded every fuckin' conversation that all of us had in our lifetime, by now each and every one of us would be fucked.

Speaking of tits, I had a woman send me an e-mail the other day. I put a thing on my Web site sayin' I was a fuckin' titty man and cordially inviting the women out there with the humongous knockers to send me a photo.

Well, one woman, bless her fuckin' heart, did so. She had 44 double-fuckin' D. I mean, *marone*! What a pair of bal-loooooooooooons! I like to howl when I say that. Bal-looooooons! Oh, my. And she had the balls to send me a fuckin' picture of 'em! *Mama mia!*

*Can you imagine the size of her fuckin' nipples? You might get a few licks in, fellas, but you ain't gettin' them titties in your mouth.*

## The Entire Government Is Corrupt

Whatever happened to good ol' honest, fuckin' government?

As I'm writing this book, the presidential elections are still almost a fuckin' year away, but already they're havin' fuckin' debates and all the candidates are takin' fuckin' potshots at each other.

One says something nasty about the other and the guy (or gal) who's just gotten slapped keeps right on smilin'. That's fuckin' politicians for you. You slap them right in the fuckin' face and they keep smiling.

I'll tell you, if I was up there in a debate and somebody started saying shit about me, I'd grab him by the fuckin' throat with one hand and knock his ass out with the other.

Now, the other night it was a dogpile on Senator Hillary Clinton. They asked her a question and she gave two different answers. How the fuck can you elect a woman like that? She wants to have everything both fuckin' ways so that nobody disagrees with her.

Well, sorry, lady, the world don't work that fuckin' way.

Now I got nothin' against Hillary Clinton but if she gets elected, you know what that means: another four years of Wild Bill in the White House. You know she's goin' to him for advice.

I mean, here's a guy who came this close to getting his ass booted out of the White House the last time he was there. The man lacks self control. Can't keep it in his fuckin' pants. What a fuckin' way to get back into the White House, have your wife get elected.

It worked for George Wallace down in Alabama years ago. They had a term limit and when Wallace had served as long as he could, his wife ran for governor, won by a landslide, and George never even switched offices.

The whole fucking government is corrupt. They're all on the fuckin' take. You know that, right? Members of Congress are trying to get money for this, money for that, money for a mule museum, money for research into why snoring couples sleep in separate rooms, and meanwhile fuckin' people are starving in this country.

I never thought I'd see a fuckin' government as corrupt as this one. It's something. They do whatever the fuck they want.

And the American people, they're all hypnotized, fuckin'

*If Hillary Clinton gets elected, you know what that means: another four years of Wild Bill in the White House.*

opiated by TV or something. They just sit there and they take it. They say, "Go ahead. Go ahead and keep pounding us up the ass with this fucking bullshit. We don't fuckin' care. We fuckin' like it."

I know I'm gettin' holed. I know that. When Nancy Pelosi starts lookin' good to me, I know I am takin' it up the ass hard and deep. She's startin' to look like a real sexy woman to me. No fuckin' doubt about it. My time is fuckin' near.

# Tommy Malone and the Bag o' Burning Horseshit

I remember Halloween back when I was growing up a kid in Brooklyn. We didn't have all them fuckin' costumes like they buy today. No fuckin' way. We couldn't afford that shit. Back then, we had to make do.

The only costume I ever had was I'd get one of my mother's nylon stockings and pull it over my head. Couldn't afford nothin' else. Then we'd go around: "Trick or treat. Treat or treat." If they didn't give us anything, we'd throw eggs at the rat bastards.

We'd put paint on their house. I mean, we were full of mischief. Full of fuckin' mischief.

I remember one time my friend Tommy Malone, he put a bag of fuckin' horseshit in front of some lady's house, poured some lighter fluid on it, and then set the motherfucker on fire. Holy shit, what a stink.

The fuckin' lady came out of the house and started stompin' out the fire and all that horseshit went all over her shoes. We laughed so hard we almost busted a fuckin' gut. I remember it like it was fuckin' yesterday.

We had fun and it didn't cost fuckin' nothin'. Not like

today, when the parents buy expensive costumes for their kids on Halloween. They'll shell out five hundred bucks for a fuckin' costume. They say, "Sure, what's the fuckin' difference?"

What happened to the fuckin' good old days when we didn't have no fuckin' money? Kids'd take a fuckin' sheet and cut holes in it so they could walk around being ghosts. "Booooo! Boooooo!"

Some of the costumes today they look so fuckin' professional, it's like the cast of a fuckin' Broadway play is wanderin' around the fuckin' neighborhood. Still I think it's a great holiday. I still love Halloween.

I buy candy for al the kiddies when they come around. Trouble is, when I answer the fuckin' door, they run like fuckin' rats. They say, "Trick or treat!" I say, "What the fuck do you want, kids? Booooo! Boooooo!" They see the size of me, they're gone.

*The fuckin' lady came out of the house and started stompin' out the fire and all that horse-shit went all over her shoes.*

## Is There Homosexuality in the Animal Kingdom?

I got nothin' against gay people but I was wonderin' the other day: Is there such a thing as gay animals? They got gay cats, lickin' each other's pussy? Gay elephants, givin' each other a little trunk? Are there gay hippopotomuses? Anybody ever see two dogs blowin' each other?

Any of you readers know? I mean it ain't a fuckin' obsession with me or nothin' like that, but I want to know. Drop me a line, send me an e-mail if anyone knows. Are there ho-mosexual practices among animals?

Is homosexuality exclusive to fuckin' humans? Anyone know? Anywhere in the world, Africa, South America, fuckin' China. They got gay mice? Gay snakes?

I think it would be a riot. Imagine seeing two eight-hundred-pound gorillas fuckin' each other up the fuckin' ass.

*Anybody ever see two dogs blowin' each other?*

## Where Did All the Cash Money Go?

You ever notice that there ain't no cash money no more? Where the fuck did it go? The only people with cash money anymore are the fuckin' drug dealers. Pushers got a wad on 'em that'll choke a fuckin' horse, but that's about it.

It's all fuckin' plastic today. Fuckin' plastic. I was in a fuckin 7-Eleven the other day and a woman in there was using a fuckin' credit card to buy an item that cost a buck ninety-two. A fuckin' buck ninety-two.

Nobody's got no fuckin' cash today. I think we're headed for some seriously bad times. I think the next fuckin' holiday season is going to be the worst all time for the fuckin' retailers out there.

Where did all the cash go? Somebody must have it. I know I ain't got it. Things are fucked up. The economy is completely fucked. Four dollars a gallon for gasoline. A dollar a fuckin' pound for fuckin' potatoes. Five dollars a pound for Black Angus.

Anybody out there know where all the cash money is, let me know. I'd like to get some!

Do you people remember when a buck was a buck? What can you do with a fuckin' buck anymore—wipe your fuckin' ass? A buck today ain't worth the fuckin' paper it's printed on.

Did you ever go into a fuckin' supermarket with a fuckin' dollar bill in your hand? You might as well roll that bill up nice and tight and shove it up your fuckin' ass, for all the fuckin' good it's gonna do ya.

You go to a movie theater and you go to the concession counter, you can't get fuckin' nothin' for a buck no more. You go to the baseball park, you go to the concession stand, you can't get nothin' for a dollar.

The dollar used to be huge but it shrank. It shrank like a fuckin' dick packed on ice. You can't even get your fuckin' shoes shined for a buck no more. You can't even buy a good roll of terlit paper.

Something's goin' on out there. Oh yeah, something is going on. When all of them foreign countries in Europe and Canada, have currency that's worth more than the American dollar, then somethin' is goin' on.

Something must be up. How can the most powerful country in the fuckin' universe have currency that ain't worth fucking shit? They should stop printing the fuckin' dollar bill. Ain't worth it no more. Print five-dollar bills. That should be the new fuckin' minimum.

*What can you do with a fuckin' buck anymore—wipe your fuckin' ass?*

## In These Biblical Times, Insurance Companies Are Lookin' for Loopholes

I tell ya, these are fuckin' biblical times. We got the wrath of fuckin' God goin' on out there. The Big Man night have to build a fuckin' ark before this shit is through. You never can tell. Droughts in Georgia. Wildfires in California. Tsunamis in Asia. Hurricanes wiping out cities along the Gulf Coast. A fuckin' tornado in Brooklyn!

A twister! The first one in Brooklyn in a hundred and eighteen fuckin' years! Uh-oh. Sodom and fuckin' Gomorrah time. Back in my day, the worst weather you had to worry about was a fuckin' snowstorm. It's that fuckin' global warming, I'm tellin' ya. Are we sure it wasn't fuckin' al Qaeda and the fuckin' Taliban pissin' on us? Was it an Iraqi fart? Holy fuckin' shit. I ain't fuckin' kiddin' this time. The world really is comin' to a fuckin' end. No shit.

It's like the ol' comic Red Buttons used to say, "Strange things are happenin'."

I feel sorry for them people in California. A fire starts fifty fuckin' miles away and when you get home from fuckin' work, your fuckin' house has burned to the ground and you got fuckin' nothin'.

I'll tell you one thing you can bet on. The insurance companies don't fuckin' wanna pay for any of this shit. No fuckin' way. They got suits staying up all fuckin' night, workin' double shifts, schemin'.

Those assholes in suits are trying to figure out ways to screw the people who lost houses out of gettin' any insurance money. That's the way the bastards are. They stay up all fuckin' night, lookin' for fuckin loopholes.

Don't you worry. They'll come up with a fuckin' excuse not to pay. During all of these natural catastrophes, you ever see one story on TV about insurance adjusters rushing to the scene to help people fuckin' rebuild?

No, me neither. That's the way it is on fuckin' insurance commercials. The guy is always there before the house stops smolderin' with a fuckin' check in his hand, but in real life they get nothin'—nothin' but fuckin' excuses, that is.

We can't let 'em get away with it. The government has got to step in and do something. They've got to keep their fuckin' eyes on the insurance companies, make sure they pay the fuck up. It's fuckin' bullshit.

These people have been paying high fuckin' premiums for their fuckin' insurance for forty fuckin' years and when they lose their fuckin' houses, the insurance companies better fuckin' pay up. Come on, you rat bastard insurance companies. Pay the fuck up. Let's go.

*The insurance companies don't fuckin' wanna pay for any of this shit. No fuckin' way.*

## The Day Jimmy the Printer Took Me to a French Whore

I remember it like it was fuckin' yesterday. Ahhhhh . . . the summer of 1963. President Kennedy is in the White House. Jan and Dean are singin' fuckin' "Surf City" on the transister radio. Surf city, here we fuckin' come. And I'm hangin' out in front of my house in Canarsie. It's hot.

Just then Jimmy the Printer pulls up in his fuckin' T-Bird convertible.

"Hey, kid, get in," he says. So I get in. "Kid, I just won $25,000 at Fat Andy's sigarette game. I'm takin' you down to get a French whore."

Sigarette is an Italian card game they used to play back in them days. It was sort of like "Bankers and Brokers."

So Jimmy the Printer takes me over to Manhattan. Fifty-fifth Street and Second Avenue. A high-rise apartment building. We go into the lobby there and we tell the doorman we want apartment 22D.

He says, "That's a thousand dollars. You can tip the girls upstairs."

That's five hundred dollars each. Holy shit. You know how much money that was back in them days? It was a fuckin' fortune. But for Jimmy the Printer, it was no fuckin' problem. He pulls out a fuckin' G-note and gives it to the guy.

So we go up to Apartment 22D and Jimmy the Printer gives another two hundred to the madam that answers the door. She tells us to pick out any broad we want.

I want to tell you, I was a kid in a candy store. How do you fuckin' pick? Each broad was better lookin' than the next. And they were French. Built. What fuckin' construction. Marvels of fuckin' nature. You had perpetual motion machines and you had your antigravity machines. It was like science fuckin' fiction only it made your dick harder than Roberto Duran's fist. Every single one of these unbelievable broads was fuckin' French. Didn't speak no English. They communicated using the universal language. But how do you pick?

Finally I picked one out. Her name is Fifi. I tell ya, in Canarsie the only thing we had named Fifi was Ol' Lady Horowitz's fuckin' poodle, the one with the two fuckin' assholes. So me and Fifi, we got along good. We had a couple of glasses of

**This is Mike the Steamfitter from Jackson Heights, Queens. A cheap bastard. He once shit in a shoebox so he wouldn't have to blow a dime on a pay toilet. (photo courtesy U.S. Attorney's Office, Eastern District of New York)**

wine. Jimmy the Printer gave me two hundred bucks to tip the babe, and she liked that. I want to tell you, she treated me real nice. Re-ee-ee-ee-al nice. She moved slow and she was gentle and she smelled better than anything I ever smelled before, like early morning on the west side of Prospect Park before anyone had walked their dog.

It was the best fuckin' sex I ever had in my fuckin' life. I was only fuckin' sixteen years old and I was in this room with red fuckin' wallpaper and a babe who looked like she should have been doin' the fuckin' cancan in the fuckin' Moulin Rouge.

And I learned something that day, something that has stuck with me for the rest of my life. I learned it's fuckin' great to have sex with a woman who can't speak and can't understand a single word of fuckin' English.

Fifi and English didn't share the same fuckin' brain. When she made sounds, it was always like, "Poco pooka pooka." Like French baby talk. When I was givin' her the beef injection, she even moaned and groaned in fuckin' French.

"Pooka pooka," she gasped.

What a fuckin' riot. You can say all the fuckin' nasty shit you want and she thinks you're sweet-talkin' her. If you tried saying that shit at home to your wife or your girlfriend, she'd hit you over the fuckin' head with a fuckin' frying pan and kick you the fuck out of your fuckin' house.

I love Par-eee in the springtime, and the summer, and the fall . . . *Chantez l'amour!*

> *Fifi and English didn't share the same fuckin' brain. When she made sounds, it was always like, "Poco pooka pooka." Like French baby talk.*

## Irish Joe Walsh Knew What Law Enforcement Was All About

You know, growing up in Brooklyn back in the fifties, people were much tougher in them days. Especially the cops.

There was one cop in particular in Canarsie that you didn't fuck with, if you were smart.

His name was Irish Joe Walsh. He was six foot fuckin' four, two hundred and thirty-five pounds of fuckin' rock. His hands were so fuckin' big he looked like he was wearin' a pair of fuckin' catcher's mitts.

Nobody fucked with Irish Joe the Cop. The cops in them days drove around two cops in a squad car. And they had no air-conditioning in them cars in the summer. When Irish Joe got out of that fuckin' cruiser and he banged that fuckin' nightstick on the fuckin' sidewalk and you didn't fuckin' move, he'd come over and poke ya.

If you said one fuckin' word to Joe the Cop, one fuckin' word, he'd bat the fuckin' shit out of you. I know what youse is thinkin': Police brutality! Police brutality! But that's fuckin' bullshit. We didn't have police brutality.

Back in Brooklyn in my time, there was no such fuckin' thing as police brutality. It didn't exist. Sure, the police were fuckin' brutal, but we didn't call it police brutality. We called it law enforcement. We called it protecting the fuckin' public safety.

Back in them days, you'd have women park their baby strollers—with the baby in it!—out in front of the store while they went inside to shop. Nobody ever stole a fuckin' baby. Not fuckin' once. If the baby started cryin', someone would go in the store and say, "Hey lady, your baby is cryin'," and she'd go out and take care of it. Nobody would even think of taking a baby out of a baby carriage.

There were no fuckin' drug dealers. There were no fuckin' hoodlums. That's because the cops back then, they ruled with a fuckin' iron fist.

The cops today, they get no fuckin' respect. They pull someone over for a traffic violation and they ask you for a driver's license and registration and, right away, they're catching grief.

"You're stopping me because I'm black!" "You're stopping me

because I'm a fuckin' Arab cocksucker!" Whatever the fuck it is. Right away, people start givin' the cop all kinds of bullshit. They say, "Let me see your badge number, I'm gonna report you."

Do you know what would have happened to you if you did that to fuckin' Joe the Cop? Do you know what would have happened if you'd asked Joe the Cop to see his fuckin' badge number? He'd grab you by the fuckin' neck, pull you out of that fuckin' car, and give you the fuckin' beating of your fucking life.

He'd say, "You still want my fuckin' badge number? Get the fuck out of here."

The cops today, they get no fuckin' respect. I remember one time my friend Tommy Malone's father, Old Man Malone, he says, "Big Mike, come to the gas station with me, I want to fill up."

I get in the car with him. When we get to the fuckin' corner, Old Man Malone doesn't stop at the stop sign, he fucking rolllllllls through it. All of a sudden, we hear the fuckin' siren and it's fuckin' Joe the Cop. Joe the Cop wants to see his driver's license and registration.

Old Man Malone starts givin' him some fuckin' lip. "Joe, you fuckin' known me for forty years, what the fuck do you want to see my license and registration for?"

Joe the Cop writes the fuckin' summons, throws it right through the fuckin' window, and says, "Have a nice day, Mr. Malone. Go fuck yourself!"

*Sure, the police were fuckin' brutal, but we didn't call it police brutality. We called it law enforcement.*

Old Man Malone turns to me and he says, "Did you see what he did, Mike? Did you see what he did? He wrote me a fuckin' summons and told me to go fuck myself!"

I said, "You're lucky. He forgot to give you the fuckin' beatin'. Let's get the fuck outa here. Let's get some fuckin' gas."

Anyway, that's the way it was back in my day. Give the cops some fuckin' respect, you rat bastards.

## Remember Anna Nicole

Hey, remember that Anna Nicole case? Seems like a long fuckin' time ago now, right? For weeks—weeks!—that was the only fuckin' thing you could get on TV. Kept us distracted from the fuckin' war in Iraq and the way everything is for shit these days.

There was a judge in that case named Judge Larry Seidlin. Remember him? Bald guy. Wept like a fuckin' baby. I got a problem with judges that fuckin' cry. Would Judge Kenesaw Mountain Landis cry? Would Judge Crater cry? Would Judge Reinhold cry? No fuckin' way. Judges got to be tough—but this one was a fuckin' mushpot.

Anyway, this Seidlin got a lawyer named Millstein to represent the interests of Baby Danilyn, to watch over the baby. Oh, Millstein watched over her all right. He charged her a hundred and seventy-five grand, the fuckin' rat bastard.

She wasn't even one years old. Ga-ga goo-goo. That takes some fuckin' balls, to charge a baby that much money. What a fuckin' shyster. A guy like that gives a legitimate lawyer a fuckin' bad name.

That Millstein got a sweet fuckin' deal. He got a free trip to the fuckin' Bahamas, charged all of his expenses to the kid. If the Florida Bar Association had any fuckin' grapefruits, they'd disbar the motherfucker.

One hundred and seventy-five thousand dollars! Do you

> *That Rita fucking Crosby. Now,*
> *there's a fuckin' desperate*
> *woman.*

know what he'd fuckin' have to do for me, to earn that kind of fuckin' scratch? He'd have to come and wipe my ass every time I was done takin' a shit!

You know who was the biggest fucking loser in that Anna Nicole bullshit? That Rita fucking Crosby. Now, there's a fuckin' desperate woman. She got herself fuckin' neck deep in donkey shit by saying a tape exists of Larry Burkhead and Howard K. Stern making love together. She wrote that in a fucking book. She said they were in a "compromising position." What is she gonna report next? Bush and Cheney got caught in a compromising position?

How the fuck did she think she was fucking gonna get away with that? You can't get away with fucking lies. You can't even get away with telling the fucking truth anymore. Dan Rather went on CBS and told the fucking truth about President Bush and they shitcanned his fucking ass on account of political pressure.

What the fuck did Rita Crosby think was going to happen to her? Did she actually hear the tape? No. She says somebody told her the fucking tape exists. Can she produce the tape? No. Prove it exists? No. She's fucked.

If I was her, I'd hang out in a cave somewhere over there in Afghanistan with fuckin' Osama bin Laden. You know who I blame? I blame the publisher. The greedy-ass publisher who let her write that fuckin' book. They should take that rat bastard and hit him over the fuckin' head with a baseball bat.

# Dead Man Fucking

I was thinkin' the other day—ohhhh, the Big Man was thinkin'—about all the condemned men on murderer's row. Condemned to die. They gotta spend fifteen, twenty years in solitary confinement. They gotta be locked up twenty-three fuckin' hours a day.

They eat fuckin' shit, and when finally all of their appeals run out they're asked, "What do you want for your last meal?"

What are they gonna give 'em? A dried-up fucking steak? Some greasy french fries? A dried-up lobster tail? Strawberry shortcake? I know, I know, these guys committed horrific crimes, but I say, give 'em a real choice.

If I was on death row on the eve of my execution, I don't think I would be all that hungry. A thing like imminent fucking death can hurt a man's appetite. I know what I would want. I'd want my last piece of ass.

I would want a fuckin' brunette, six foot tall. Forty-four double-D! Twenty-two-inch waist and a long pair of fuckin' stems. She'd be wearing spike high heels and a pair of fuckin' fishnet stockings.

She'd start off by giving me a nice slow blow job and then I'd fuck the night away. By the time I was fuckin' done with her, I would wish I was on that gurney or in that gas chamber or strapped into ol' sparky.

*Forty-four double-D! Twenty-two-inch waist and a long pair of fuckin' stems. She'd be wearing spike high heels and a pair of fuckin' fishnet stockings.*

I think death row prisoners should die with a smile on their face. I know. They committed all of this horrific crimes, but give 'em a fuckin' choice, for chrissakes: last meal or last piece of fuckin' ass.

## A Coupla Reasons to Stay North of the Border

I seen the ex-president of Mexico on that *Bill O'Reilly Show* the other day. The guy claims that 50 percent of Mexicans got to live on four dollars a day. That means that if you go to a fuckin' McDonald's down there in Mexico, it's like going to a five-star restaurant here in the United States. It's like eating at the fuckin' Ritz.

I'll tell you one thing right now, people, ain't no one gonna go to one of them fuckin' Starbucks down there in Mexico. Of course, I find it hard to believe that anyone goes to that fuckin' Starbucks here, either, but they do. Don't make no fuckin' sense to me.

The only Mexicans down there who can fuckin' afford to go to Starbucks are the fuckin' drug dealers. Four dollars a fuckin' day. Give me a fuckin' break. For four dollars a day north of the border, you couldn't even shine your fuckin' shoes. For four dollars a day, you couldn't even wipe your fuckin' ass in this country.

This guy Michael Moore, the guy that made that movie *Sicko*, he claims that the medical benefits down there in fuckin' Cuba are better than in the United States. I don't fuckin' think so, Michael Moore.

Hey, Michael Moore, anytime you or someone in your

family has got to have major surgery, why don't you fly down to fuckin' Cuba and have it done there, you fuckin' lyin' rat fuckin' bastard. Who are you fuckin' bullshittin'? You're blowin' smoke up the Americans' ass.

And how about them fuckin' pinko movie stars like Sean Penn and Kevin Spacey? They got nothin' nice to say about the United States. They'd rather break beak down there in Venezuela with that Venezuelan dictatin' pimp Hugo Chávez.

All you fuckin' movie stars out there who got something bad to say about the United States, why don't you give up your citizenship and go live someplace else? Get the fuck out!

> *Hey, Michael Moore, anytime you or someone in your family has got to have major surgery, why don't you fly down to fuckin' Cuba and have it done there, you fuckin' lyin' rat fuckin' bastard.*

## I Finally Found the World's Only Honest Newspaper

You know people, it's hard to find an honest newspaper today. There ain't one paper out there that's got proper journalism. The journalists today, they take their orders from the suits. They take their orders from the executives upstairs.

They can't write what they want. They can't write the

> *They had a fuckin' story in there about Reverend Al "the Instigator" Sharpton. Turns out he's really white. Who fuckin' knew?*

fuckin' truth. They gotta write what the corporates tell 'em to write. You might think the world is comin' to an end, but me, I finally found an honest newspaper.

The *National Enquirer!* They always fuckin' tell the truth. The other day I was reading that paper and they said that both Paris Hilton and Britney Spears are transvestites. I was skeptical at first, but it was right there in the *Enquirer*, so it must be true. (Remember that week when Paris and Britney were hangin' out together? What a pair of simps. Between the two of them, they didn't have an IQ of fifty.)

They had a fuckin' story in there about Reverend Al "the Instigator" Sharpton. Turns out he's really white. Who fuckin' knew? Must be true, because it's right there in the *Enquirer*. They say he uses black shoe polish to put the fuckin' color on.

O. J. Simpson's got cancer. I know, boo-fuckin'-hoo—but it must be true. In the *Enquirer*.

Drinkin' prune juice every day lowers your cholesterol 75 fuckin' percent. In the *Enquirer*. Must be true. I'll tell you one thing: even if drinkin' prune juice don't lower your fuckin' cholesterol by 75 percent, you'll be lookin' for a fuckin' bowl every day because you'll be shittin' your fuckin' brains out.

Who reads this fuckin' newspaper? Fuckin' people who are fuckin' brain dead? The *National Enquirer*. The fuckin' world is shot.

## There's No Such Thing as a Used Car No More

You know, growin' up in Brooklyn, I used to buy a used car. It was new to me but it was a used car. But they don't call 'em used cars no more. They call 'em pre-owned. They should use that expression in other ways, too.

For instance, you single guys out there who are thinking about marrying a divorced woman, stop thinking of her as a divorced woman and start thinking of her as pre-owned. She got a lot of miles on her. She's in pretty good shape. She spent the best years of her life with somebody else. Somebody else nibbled on them hotcakes. She's a good woman—but she's pre-owned.

The same with you women out there who are thinking of marrying a divorced man. Sure, he don't have the shine he used to have. He's set in his ways. He's a good man. He's a real good man. But he's pre-owned.

You wanna know somethin'? I wanna tell ya somethin' from the bottom of my heart. Something pre-owned can make you feel brand-new.

*She's a good woman—but she's pre-owned.*

# When a Cool Breeze Turns into a Wet Fart

Tell me if this ever happened to you. You're riding along in your car, driving, you got a couple of people with you. You feel a little gas in your stomach. So you lift a cheek and go to lay a cool breeze—but it comes out a wet fart.

It's okay. It happens to everybody, everybody in the world. You gotta little gas, go to lay a cool breeze, and it comes out a wet fart. It's okay. You know what I'm talking about, right?

You start squirming in your seat. You feel very uncomfortable. Then you see some brown liquid runnin' down your leg. You're embarrassed. The people in the car, they start complainin': "What's that smell? It smells like the fuckin' Industrial Park slaughterhouse in August! It's like, it's like a stench!"

Well, it *is* a fuckin' stench. That's what happened to me a few weeks ago. I went to lay a cool breeze and out came a wet fart. I ran into the fuckin' nearest diner to wash up and half the fuckin' joint ran out. They couldn't take the fuckin' stench. I stunk out the whole fuckin' joint—but it happens to everybody.

What are you gonna do? Cool breeze. Wet fart. That's fuckin' life.

*You start squirming in your seat. You feel very uncomfortable. Then you see some brown liquid runnin' down your leg.*

## When Will Women Learn That Men Chase Pussy?

In New York, there used to be a team that made everyone proud. They were the New York Knickerbockers and the whole town loved 'em. You had Willis Reed, and Bill Bradley, and Walt "Clyde" Frazier. They were great.

Today, the Knicks suck fuckin' moose cock and they've done so for a long time. Turns out, one of the reasons they can't play basketball anymore is because the current crop spends too much time thinkin' about getting some fuckin' poontang pie.

They got this one guy Stephon Marbury from fuckin' Coney Island, if he spent as much time practicing his crossover dribble as he did practicing pouring the fuckin' pork to interns in the back of SUVs, the Knicks might win some fuckin' basketball games.

The coach, Isiah Thomas, got convicted of sexual harassment. The Knicks gotta pay out $11.6 million. So the coach should probably think more about basketball, too, and less about hittin' on the fuckin' women in the fuckin' front office.

Now what happened to Isiah, I seen happen thirteen, fourteen years ago to Supreme Court Justice Clarence Thomas. Remember that? Anita Hill accused him of sexual harassment. Even the great Bill O'Reilly had to settle a sexual harassment suit out of court.

Even Reverend Al "the Instigator" Sharpton has gotten into the sexual harassment act. He's been known to take a whiff or two. Now, I don't know what any of them guys did or didn't do to those women, and to tell the God-honest truth, I don't give a flying fuck.

I got one fuckin' question: When are you fuckin' women going to learn? I got the utmost respect for all of you

> *If Stephon Marbury spent as much time practicing his crossover dribble as he did practicing pouring the fuckin' pork to interns in the back of SUVs, the Knicks might win some fuckin' basketball games.*

women out there, but when the fuck are you going to learn that this is what men do?

Men chase pussy! I know. I know. Some guys cross the line. Like ex-president Bill Clinton. I know. Men chase pussy. You women have got to stop being so shocked by it. That's the way it fuckin' is.

Now, I'm a male and I know that all us males are the same. There's something in us, something instinctive. When a beautiful woman is nearby, we got to look at her. We can't help it. And when she walks by, we all got to turn our heads, slow. We got to get a back view, too.

I was in a restaurant the other night and a woman walked in there. She had to be thirty, thirty-two years old. She was gorgeous! Knockdown gorgeous. She was a twin for Angelina Jolie. She had them big sexy lips, the kind of lips that remind you of that childbirth film they show on the Discovery health channel. She had a big bust and a beautiful head. She was a knockout.

I couldn't help myself. I almost fell off my fuckin' chair. She could make a fuckin' dead man fuckin' come. Every guy in that fuckin' joint turned his head to watch her walk by. And every fuckin' guy left that joint with a fuckin' hard-on.

I got to tell ya, I love them sexy women. I love to look at 'em. They turn me on.

## Where Do People Who Disappear Go?

All the fuckin' time, I see on the news stories about married couples. He's missing. She's missing. Come on, give me a fucking break. They disappeared? They disap*peared*? How can anybody fuckin' disappear?

Where do they go? I'll tell you where they go. They either go to the nearest chop shop, or they go on a fishin' expedition where they slip on a banana peel and fall overboard into the ocean. That's where they go. They get eatin' by a fuckin' shark.

They were fuckin' iced. Disappear? Disappear? They got a fuckin' ice pick behind the fuckin' ear, that's what they fuckin' got. And it's always the fuckin' wife or husband who did it. And you know why?

Because they're the only ones who fuckin' give a flying fuck, that's why. Nobody else cares enough to kill 'em. You gotta work up some serious hate to put a fuckin' ice pick behind someone's ear, and who else but a spouse is gonna hate someone that fuckin' much? Nobody.

So what the fuck is up with the news media with this "disappeared" crapola? They disappeared for fuckin' two years now? Where did they go? They put up their picture. "Did you see this woman?"

Well, disappeared, my ass. Go look in the local chop shop. You'll find her, don't worry about it.

*Disappeared, my ass. Go look in the local chop shop.*

## Husbands, Here's How to Tell When It's Time to Get Out

You know the Big Man gets a lot of e-mails, a lot of fuckin' e-mails, and many of them are from married men, guys that have been married for ten, fifteen, twenty years, and they are all fuckin' miserable.

They write and they say, "Hey, Big Man, what should I do?"

Well, this is for all you married men out there. You want to know when you get out? You want to know when to get a divorce? When you haven't seen your wife naked in more than two years and you haven't had sex with your mate in more than two years, then, fellas it is time to get the fuck out.

When you and your wife are sleepin' in separate bedrooms because separate beds ain't enough, it's time to get the fuck out.

When you sit at the fuckin' breakfast table and all you fuckin' do is eat and you don't communicate with verbal language at all, then it's time to get out.

When you go take out the fuckin' garbage and you don't come back for two hours because you don't want to go back inside and look at that sorry-ass bitch, then it is time to get out.

When you work all day, slavin' for eight fuckin' hours, and when you come home you sit in your car for two fuckin' hours before goin' inside, it's time to get the fuck out. When you no longer want to look at that bitch, fellas, it's time to take the fuckin' gas pipe.

Get the fuck out! Are you out of your fuckin' mind? I know what you're sayin'. I hear ya. You say you're hangin' in for the fuckin' kids. Get the fuck out. You ain't doin' the kids no fuckin' favor by sittin' in the car out in front of your house because you can't stomach the look of their mother. Get the fuck out, you stupid bastards.

> *When you go take out the fuckin' garbage and you don't come back for two hours because you don't want to go back inside and look at that sorry-ass bitch, then it is time to get out.*

## The Way Men and Women Think Differently

You know, men and women, we're like two different creatures. We don't think alike. No way men and women think alike. I'll give you a for-instance.

If you're walkin' in a supermarket with your wife or girlfriend, or you go to a restaurant with your wife or girlfriend, or you go to a concert, or wherever you fuckin' go with her, and she catches you staring at another woman, all fuckin' hell breaks loose. Am I right?

"What are staring at, Earl? Don't let me catch you lookin' at another woman, Earl, or I'll bust your fuckin' ass."

"I ain't starin' at nothin', baby."

"Don't give me that fuckin' bullshit. I seen you starin' at that young girl."

"No, baby. I swear. I ain't starin' at that young girl. Why would I stare at another woman, baby? You are so beautiful, baby. Why would I want to fuckin' look at another bim—, uh, woman?"

In the meantime, while you're blatherin' your fuckin' brains out trying to plead fuckin' innocent, she's lookin' around for the nearest thing to knock you over the head with.

So that's the way women think. We men, we think totally different. Totally fuckin' different.

When we take our wife or girlfriend, a woman we been with for five, ten, fifteen, twenty fuckin' years, to a restaurant, concert, bar, whatever, and we catch her lookin' at another man, we don't say a fuckin' word. We don't let loose with a fuckin' peep.

We just think to ourselves, "Please, God, please, Lord, let there be a connection here."

You are praying that she'll fuckin' fall in love so that you can get rid of the fuckin' bitch.

You're praying, "Pleeeeeease. Pleeeease. Take her! Take her the fuck off of my hands. She's yours!"

*"Don't let me catch you lookin' at another woman, Earl, or I'll bust your fuckin' ass."*

## The Big Man Has Had Some Ups and Downs

I gotta admit, I've had my share of personal problems. Years ago, lately, don't make no fuckin' difference. The Big Man's fuckin' life is right out of the fuckin' Book of Job. So, a few weeks back, I had some problems I had to take care of—out of town.

I got back and I was gettin' fuckin' phone calls from people, people I owe money to.

"We thought you ran away," they said. "We thought you was hidin' from us."

Right. People, there ain't a spot on the four corners of this Earth where the Big Man could be inconspicuous. I mean, where the fuck am I gonna fuckin' hide? Give me a fuckin' break. Where the fuck could I go?

I couldn't even hide in the fuckin' hills of Afghanistan. Fuckin' Osama bin fuckin' Laden might be able to hide in Afghanistan but the Big Man would stick out like a fuckin' Muslim woman in a thong.

No matter where I went, they would find me. A guy my fuckin' size. They got fuckin' satellites today that can take pictures of me from space. That's me right there, the guy flippin' the fuckin' bird.

Imagine if I really went fuckin' missing! Imagine a police bulletin going out on my fuckin' description. They would find me in three fuckin' minutes. Besides, the Big Man don't run from nobody. That's because I can't fuckin' run. I'm too fuckin' big.

Yeah, I guess you could figure out from that that I'm a little down on my luck. That's the way it is with the Big Man. He's got ups and downs. Right now I'm goin' through some downs. I could use some fuckin' scratch.

But how to get some dough? I tell you, it frosts my ass when I read about the commodities that are bringin' in the big bucks these days. For example, there are people willing to pay a million fuckin' bucks for the fuckin' orange jumpsuit Paris Hilton wore when she was in jail.

They're offerin' a hundred fuckin' thousand dollars for a pair of Britney Spears's soiled panties. I thought she didn't wear panties but—what do I know?—the offer is on the table. I don't know if they got to have skid marks or what. Maybe just pee stains'll do the fuckin' trick. Maybe it's extra with skid marks. A Britney Spears skid mark, that's fuckin' real dough.

Now they say fifty fuckin' thousand for a bra that Anna

A rare shot of Tommy Funzi, who ran all the rackets in Canarsie. He swore he was the inspiration for Don Corleone in *The Godfather*. He was too cheap to spring for a dead horse, so when he wanted to threaten you, he put a dead goldfish in your bed. (photo courtesy U.S. Attorney's Office, Eastern District of New York)

Nicole Smith wore. That must be some heavy-duty bra. With fuckin' support like that, you could straighten out the fuckin' Leanin' Tower of Pisa.

I mean, come on, give me a fuckin' break. Who pays this kind of fuckin' money out there? But it got me thinkin' and I came up with an idea. Here's what I'm gonna do with youse. If there's anyone out there who wants to buy a pair of the Big Man's soiled fuckin' underwear—piss stains, skid marks, whatever the fuck you want—they are for sale. How many people out there want a pair of my soiled fuckin' drawers?

If you want 'em clean, I'll fuckin' wash 'em, I'll fuckin' dry 'em, and I'll fuckin' fold 'em. Up to you. I'll even fuckin' autograph 'em for you. Twenty-five dollars! I need the fuckin' money. And remember, consider this, if you get tired of the mother-fuckers, you can always sell them to al fuckin' Qaeda, you can always sell them to the fuckin' Taliban, to use as a fuckin' parachute! Geronimo!

That's not all I fuckin' got for sale. Check this out! Step right up, ladies and gentlemen, tell you what I'm gonna do. I'll throw in a pair of my wife Mona's bloomers. You can get 'em in two styles: solid black and multi-fuckin'-colored, guaranteed to have warmed Mona's ass. Twenty-five fuckin' bucks.

Now I know what you are thinkin'. What would anyone want with a seventy-one-year-old woman's bloomers. Well, my Mona might be seventy-one years old, but she's only twenty-eight under the fuckin' sheets!

Take it from the Big Man, fellas, women are like a fine bottle of wine. The older the wine gets, the better it gets. And I'm gonna go one better.

I tell ya what. I'll sweeten the fuckin' deal. I'm gonna offer a fuckin' two-for-one sale. Both the Big Man's drawers and my Mona's bloomers, and I'm gonna practically give 'em away for a fuckin' forty-nine ninety-five, postage included.

I tell ya, I'm desperate for fuckin' money!

*Fuckin' Osama bin fuckin' Laden might be able to hide in Afghanistan but the Big Man would stick out like a fuckin' Muslim woman in a thong.*

# What Happened to All the Mortgage Companies?

Hey, did you see what happened to all the mortgage companies? They went down faster than Paris Hilton wearin' knee pads. Whatcha got now is a buyer's market. Wanna buy a house? You can get one fuckin' cheap. Nobody's payin' his fuckin' mortgage no more.

You know who's next? The credit card companies. Who can pay their credit card bill these days? I know I can't. Ever see the interest these credit card companies charge these days? Who the fuck can pay?

These companies, they give people all kinds of credit, give 'em all kinds of money, and—fuckin' surprise!—the people can't fuckin' pay. What I wanna know is, who the fuck is gonna end up payin' all these bills?

I can't even afford to buy a turkey sandwich for Thanksgiving, let alone a whole fuckin' turkey. These credit card companies are gonna fold up like a ton o' fuckin' bricks. You mark my words. It's getting to the fuckin' point where I can't even afford a pair of shoelaces!

Here's another one: I ain't got a master's degree in economics or nothin' like that, so if you can figure this one out let me know, it's got me goin' fuckin' crazy. It's the airlines. How do they stay in business?

The airlines say they are losing millions of dollars every year. Year after year. But they stay in business. How the fuck does that work? If I opened a diner and it cost more than it made, I'd have to close up shop. How come the airlines just keep goin' and goin' and goin' like the fuckin' Energizer Bunny?

The airlines are fuckin' leakier than a beer drinker with a swollen prostate. I mean they're billions in the fuckin' red. So what do the corporate fat cats do? They give everyone, the pilots, the stewardesses, the mechanics, everyone, a fuckin' decrease in pay.

Everyone gets docked 25 fuckin' percent. But do the fat cats decrease their own fuckin' pay? No fuckin' way. That would be un-American. They get a fuckin' raise. Their perks get bigger and bigger.

Their salary goes up, up, up, and everyone else's salary goes down, down, down. So if you're wonderin' where the fuckin' billion dollars is goin', first place to look is under the mattress of the fuckin' CEO.

Are they better than all the nice folks who work for the airlines? How come the head corporate bastards got a fuckin' license to steal? They ought to get fuckin' indicted by the fuckin' FBI because that's what they're doin', robbin' everybody blind.

> *What I wanna know is, who the fuck is gonna end up payin' all these bills?*

## Justice Is So Swift It Only Took 'Em Four Years to Indict Barry Bonds

I was readin' the fuckin' newspaper the other day. Imagine that? A newspaper! Remember them? They're obsolete now, like the horse and buggy but, back in the old days, a lot of people used to read 'em. Today, when you get the newspaper, the news is already a day and a half old. The only thing a newspaper is good for today is pickin' up the dog shit.

I know the chances that you read the fuckin' newspaper

are somewheres between slim and none; today, you get your fuckin' news from me. Here's your ace fuckin' reporter Mike Caracciolo with the fuckin' Kid from Brooklyn news.

As I write this, they just fuckin' indicted Barry Bonds. Well, that was quick. It only took 'em four years. Four years! They had to wait until after he broke the fuckin' home-run record before pulling the trigger? And the charges: perjury and obstruction of justice.

If that sounds familiar, those were the charges against Bill Clinton—and Martha fuckin' Stewart, while you're at it.

The Big Man, if you want to know the truth, doesn't give a flying fuck if Barry Bonds used steroids. He used 'em, he didn't use 'em, all the same difference to me. It still takes hand-eye coordination to hit the fuckin' ball and ain't no steroids gonna give you that. Back in my time, they had a home-run hitter by the name of Mickey Mantle.

Mantle used to get fuckin' stoned the night before the game. Played with a hangover. On one hot summer afternoon, the fuckin' Yankee manager back then, the ol' fuckin' perfessor Casey Stengel discovered Mickey Mantle asleep on the bench, trying to sleep it off.

Stengel shook Mantle and told him to wake the fuck up, go in there, and hit. Mantle rubbed his eyes, grabbed a fuckin' bat, and stepped onto the field. He hit the first pitch for a home run, jogged with a light limp—on account of he had crummy knees—around the bases, returned to the dugout, and promptly fell the fuck back asleep on the bench. True fuckin' story. You could look it up.

Now, you gonna call booze a fuckin' performance-enhancing drug? Give me a break with these fuckin' steroids these days. I'm sick of hearing about it.

In other fuckin' so-called news, Lindsay Lohan, a repeat offender, does eighty-four minutes in the Los Angeles County Jail. There's some more justice. You wouldn't want to incarcerate her longer than that; she's got a nightclub to go to, after all. She's a fuckin' drunk driver.

O. J. Simpson. That's right. O. J. Simpson. He's on fuckin' trial again. Makes me feel kind of nostalgic for that night I was tryin' to watch the fuckin' Knicks game and the only thing on was O.J. in his fuckin' Bronco.

I'm tellin' ya, I don't even think O.J.'s fuckin' lawyers are gonna make a buck on that deal. The only winners with O.J. goin' back on trial are TV news and the tabloids. I mean, who gives a fuck about O.J. anymore?

People today are desperate for cash. They'll do anything for money. And I mean fuckin' anything. I can't believe it. I mean look at that fuckin' book that O.J. put out: *If I Did It.* (We know he fuckin' did it.) They should take the publisher of that fuckin' book and hit her over the head with a fuckin' crowbar.

That O.J. has got to be the luckiest guy on the face of the Earth. He beat a double murder rap. So he's free to commit armed robbery. That O.J. must have a brain the size of a fuckin' pea. He's got to be the dumbest rat bastard in the whole fuckin' world.

There are people who think O.J. has been "livin' large" since he got away with murder. I don' know about that, folks. If you want to know about O.J.'s lifestyle, just take a look at where he was stayin' in Las Vegas when this caper came down.

He and his cronies were stayin' at the Palace Station Hotel. That ain't exactly the Bellagio, you know. That's a joint where they got a $1.99 buffet. That's where they send all the fuckin' bustouts. Fuckin' Reverend Al goes there because you can get all the fuckin' grease you can eat for a fucking buck ninety-nine. You know Reverend Al, right? He's the fuckin' guy that likes to light two sticks of dynamite at once just to see which one is gonna fuckin' blow up first.

At the Palace Station, the rooms are $14.99 a night. That's where you go if you want to pick up a lady of the evening.

For another twenty fuckin' bucks, you can get your fuckin' monkey polished and leave.

The Palace Station is the sort of a joint where they change the fuckin' bedsheet twice a fuckin' week, no matter how many people have been in and out of the fuckin' room spilling their various bodily juices and excretions. Exterminator comes in once a month, squirts some shit into the corners.

That's where O.J. stayed. Not livin' large. Another thing that amazes me about O.J. is that he has friends at all. I mean, would you stay overnight in a hotel with him? Even a nice hotel? You would have to be out of your fuckin' mind.

Britney Spears gets in another fuckin' car accident, that makes three this fuckin' week—but the good news is, this time, she didn't have the fuckin' kids in the car. See? She is growing up. She is becoming fucking responsible.

And here's the topper, the absolute fuckin' topper: The Golden Boy, Oscar de la Hoya, is a cross-dresser. Did you see them pictures of him on the fuckin' Internet in his fishnet stockings, high heels, and panties? Holy shit.

Anyway, that's the shit they got on the news these days. You got to be a celebrity who's fucking up to get in the newspaper or on TV. I think the fuckin' news media is just trying to get us to look this way so we won't look that way.

Look at all of the stories that aren't getting reported. Here's the story I want to see: "Tonight at eleven, the true power behind the Bush administration." That might garner some fucking ratings.

Who controls the White House? What special-interest group pulls the fucking strings? Does it matter who wins the presidency of the United States? Is the fuckin' president really just a fuckin' puppet for corporate America?

Look at the economy today. We're in the worst economy ever. The housing market is in the fuckin' shithole. People are fuckin' maxed out on their fuckin' credit cards. And the

U.S. government, whoever the fuck is running it, makes a thousand a day and spends a million a day.

Where's all that fuckin' money gonna come from? But is TV news warnin' ya, are they tellin' ya that the whole thing is gonna come crashing down like a ton o' bricks? No way. No time. O.J. is fuckin' on trial again.

And Britney flashed her fuckin' pussy. Again.

That's all that fuckin' matters.

> *Britney Spears gets in another fuckin' car accident, that makes three this fuckin' week—but the good news is, this time, she didn't have the fuckin' kids in the car. See? She is growing up.*

## An Evening in Giuseppe's Fine Italian Cuisine

I went to an Italian restaurant the other night: Giuseppe's Fine Italian Cuisine. I knew right away, as soon as I walked in, that I was in the wrong fucking joint. They had an open kitchen. You could see right into the fuckin' kitchen.

Don't get me wrong. I'm not a prejudiced guy. I like everybody. But in that kitchen were five Mexican guys cookin' up the fuckin' food. Five Mexicans. There was a Chinese guy washing the fucking dishes. There was a Hasidic Jew waitin' on the fuckin' tables.

Fine Italian cuisine? The food tasted like fuckin' shit! It

was like eatin' fuckin' dog food out of the fuckin' can. When I go in an Italian restaurant, I want to see a fuckin' Italian someplace, you know what I mean?

I mean, would you want to go into a Jewish deli and see five fuckin' Muslims behind the counter making fuckin' corned beef sandwiches? Even the Italians don't wanna fuckin' work no more. They're gettin' fuckin' Mexicans to do their fuckin' cookin'.

> *I mean, would you want to go into a Jewish deli and see five fuckin' Muslims behind the counter making fuckin' corned beef sandwiches?*

## The Entrepreneurial Girls of Canarsie, 1963

I was reminiscin' the other day—rem-o-niscin'—thinkin' back to the old days in Brooklyn, when I was fifteen, sixteen years old, and we used to hang out with a girl by the name of Ann Marie Hanratty. Maybe you read about her in my first book (called *Go F\*\*\* Yourself*, makes a great holiday present!).

Ann Marie's father was Tommy Hanratty. He was a big man. A construction worker. He had hands on him bigger than a pair of glazed hams—all freckled and scarred from feeding knuckle sandwiches to assholes who looked at him funny.

I must've seen that guy a thousand times in my life and every time he had a bottle of Ballantine beer in his hand.

Sometimes he was standin' up. Sometimes sittin' down. But always—always!—with a fuckin' bottle of Ballantine.

Most of the time when we went over there to pick up his daughter, he'd be sittin' in a chair there in the living room, watching *Bonanza* or *Gunsmoke* or some such, and he'd say, "Goin' out with my Ann Marie tonight, boys? Well, don't do anything I wouldn't do! You wouldn't want to fuck with the Irish, would you, boys?"

Well, we could tell that this guy had no clue. No fuckin' clue. Because, as some of you already know, Ann Marie Hanratty was better known on the streets of Canarsie as "Hand-job Annie." For two fuckin' bucks, she'd give you a whack job.

Don't do anything I wouldn't do! Unless Ann Marie was polishing her old man's monkey, that wasn't gonna happen! We used to take Annie over there to East 92nd Street into the alley next to Scrappy's Candy Store.

I'll never forget as long as I live, one night I seen Hand-job Annie take Louis Lombardi back in the alley and give him a stroke job. Louis came out and said, "That Hand-job Annie, she can stroke ya better than one of Scrappy's fuckin' milk shakes."

That Louis Lombardi was a cheap fuckin' bastard. So if he was shellin' out the two bucks for a hand job, you knew there was some quality in the technique.

Then there was Mary "Melons" Cloninger. She also knew how to make boys happy. Mary Cloninger had these humon-

*Louis came out and said, "That Hand-job Annie, she can stroke ya better than one of Scrappy's fuckin' milk shakes."*

gous fuckin' tits. But she didn't deal in cash. She was more interested in her stomach. If you bought her a pastry at the bakery shop, she'd take out those big boobs and let you feel those big ol' titties all over. *Marone!*

Those were the days. Don't seem likely I'll see days like that again.

## I'd Rather Be Blind Drunk Than Shit-Faced Any Day

Did you ever wonder where they got some of those old-time expressions? Like "meathead." A meathead's a guy who's got a box of rocks upstairs. Elevator don't make it all the way to the fuckin' penthouse.

Or how about "nutjob"? The guy's crazy. You stay away from him. The guy's a nut.

Or how about the expression "penny-pincher"? He drains every fuckin' penny out of ya and then won't let loose with a penny. A penny-pincher is a real cheap bastard.

Did you ever wonder where they got the expression "blind drunk"? If you're sittin' in a cocktail lounge or a bar and it's three thirty in the morning and the bartender says, "Last call"— this goes for both men and women—and you're kind of horny and you order the last drink of the night and you're lookin' all around to find someone to take home to have sex with and you wake up the next morning and the person you're lying next to ain't got no teeth in their mouth and they ain't got no hair on their head and they make Rosie O'Donnell look like a fuckin' beauty queen—well, that, my friends, is blind fuckin' drunk.

Now they got the term "shit-faced." It's the same thing,

goin' to a bar, pickin' up somebody, having sex with 'em, and wakin' up in the morning, goin' to take a piss, lookin' in the bathroom mirror, and you got shit all over your face.

I tell ya, fellas, you know what that is? That means you had your tongue up the wrong fuckin' hole all night. I'd rather be blind drunk than shit-faced any day of the fuckin' week!

*Fellas, that means you had your tongue up the wrong fuckin' hole all night.*

## Back When the TV Screen Was Almost Round and Eight Inches Across

Today you got high-definition TV and flat screens the size of a fuckin' movie screen, takes up on whole fuckin' wall of the living room. I remember back in the old days when I was a kid in the early fifties.

The TVs back then had a screen that was almost round, and maybe eight inches across, tops. The whole family would gather around that black-and-white television set. It wasn't cheap, either. Even back then, it would cost four, five hundred bucks. That was real fuckin' money. Not everybody had a fuckin' TV and them that did had only one. Today you got a fuckin' TV in every room, but back then there was one, it was in the living room, and everyone sat around and watched the same thing at the same fuckin' time.

There was no remote control, either. You wanted to change

> *He even had a fuckin' TV set
> in the fuckin' bathroom. You
> couldn't even take a fuckin' shit
> in peace.*

the channel, you had to get up off your fuckin' ass and turn the dial, click, click, click. You only had a handful of stations to choose from, not like the hundred you got today.

And you know what? Families got close that way. We got close to one another. Today, TV pulls families apart. I went out to see a friend of mind the other day, lives out there on Long Island, got a twelve-room house, a TV in every fuckin' room.

He even had a fuckin' TV set in the fuckin' bathroom. You couldn't even take a fuckin' shit in peace. Sittin' there, tryin' to take a dump and fat black women are slappin' one another on *Jerry* fuckin' *Springer*.

What happened to the good old days when you had one TV set and everyone gathered around? Families laughed together. They cried together. That's the problem today. We got too many things.

Everybody's got his own TV. Everybody's got his own fuckin' bathroom. Everybody's got his own fuckin' car. Listen to me, bring back them good old days. There ain't nothin' like lookin' at *The Honeymooners* on a black-and-white eight-inch screen.

## Just Friends

I was readin' the fuckin' newspaper about six weeks ago and they had this story. Cops caught this man and this woman having sex in a public rest room.

Cop asked them, "Are you boyfriend and girlfriend?"

"No," they said. "We're just good friends."

Come on! Give me a fuckin' break! You're fuckin' screwin' in a fuckin' men's room and you got the balls to tell the cops that you're just fuckin' friends. But that's the fuck the way it is in this day and age.

I went to a wedding last week. I was sitting there and this guy and girl at my table were holding hands.

I asked the guy, "Hey, you goin' out with each other?"

"No," he said. "We're just good friends."

Just friends, my fuckin' ass! Do friends screw each other? I mean, I don't know. I really don't know. That's why I'm askin'. You tell me. I'm gettin' fuckin' old. What the fuck do I know anymore?

Here ya are, having sexual intercourse three fuckin' nights a fuckin' week and you're just fuckin' friends. I wish I had friends like that when I was fuckin' growin' up. *Marone!* What a fuckin' world that would have been.

> *You're fuckin' screwin' in a fuckin' men's room and you got the balls to tell the cops that you're just fuckin' friends.*

## Ladies, Give Your Man What He Really Wants

This one is for all you ladies out there. Is it your man's birthday? Did he get a promotion at work? Is it a special occasion for your man? Are you tired of giving him the same old necktie, the same old shirt, or maybe buyin' him some flowers?

Call 1-800-HOOKERS. We got the best dickie suckers in the country. We got 'em big and small, short and tall. We got 'em white, black, Asian, and Chinese. Jewish, Italian, we got every kind. From 32B to 44 double-D. Blondes! Brunettes! Redheads! The greatest hookers in the world. This year, give your man something he'll really enjoy. Just dial 1-800-HOOKERS and tell 'em the Big Man sent ya.

## Wakes Ain't Like They Used to Be

I went to a wake last week, went over there to the funeral parlor. I wanna tell ya, wakes ain't like when I was growin' up in Brooklyn in the fifties. Back then, a widow wore a black dress to the wake. In fact, she wore a black dress from then on. She put it on when her husband died and she kept it on until the day she died.

Last week, I went over there to see Eddie the Pollack. The poor bastard dropped dead, forty-nine years old, of a heart attack. He had a wife and three kids. He worked three jobs to support his family. He dropped dead just like that. Just like that!

There was Eddie the Pollack's wife in the fuckin' funeral parlor, wearin' a beautiful red dress. She looked like she was going to a fucking opening in fucking Hollywood. Hair, makeup, all gorgeous, flirtin' with all the men.

Flirtin' with the funeral parlor guys, even! Give me a fuckin' break. Eddie the Pollack ain't even completely chilled off yet. He wasn't even in the fuckin' hole and his wife was flirting her brains out with the fuckin' morticians! She was lookin' to pick up some guy.

The thing that got me most were the people comin' up to the fuckin' coffin.

"Oooooh, he looks good. He looks so good, Charlie. Eddie looks so good."

Of course, he looks good! He's fucking dead! A makeup artist made him look that good, you stupid bastards.

*Eddie the Pollack wasn't even completely chilled off yet and his wife was flirting her brains out with the fuckin' morticians!*

## Fellas, Don't Call a Girl a Whore Unless You Mean It in the Nice Way

You know what bothers me a lot? It's when I hear a guy call a woman a whore. Back in Brooklyn, when I was a teenager, some of my best friends were whores. The best times I ever had, my greatest all-time times, were with whores.

When the Big Man went out on a Friday or Saturday night, I wasn't lookin' for a nice girl. I wasn't lookin' for the kind of girl I could bring home to Mom. I wasn't lookin' for a girl who could cook a seven-course meal while wearing white gloves.

No. I was lookin' for a good, old-fashioned whore. You know the type. You know what I'm talkin' about. These were girls who'd fuck for a week because you bought her a slice of pizza and a Coke. Buy her an ice cream and she'd give you blow jobs for another week.

It's not like today. These were girls who understood the value of a blow job. Ahhhhh, a good old-fashioned whore. So, this is to all you young fellas out there: when you take a girl out on a date on a Friday or Saturday night, and you take her to a show and you take her to dinner and it costs you three, four hundred dollars and at the end of the night she gives you a fuckin' little peck on the fuckin' cheek and you go home with a fuckin' case of the fuckin' blue balls, remember what I'm tellin' ya.

There's nothin' like a good old-fashioned whore, fellas. When you take a whore out on a date, you're goin' home with a smile on your face. Give me a fuckin' whore any day of the week.

*It's not like today. These were girls who understood the value of a blow job.*

## The Jug Man Is Always Happy to See Ya

The Big Man gets a lot of e-mails. Thousands a day. Some of 'em say, "You fat, old cocksucker!" Well, I may be fat and I may be old but you can bet your life—you heard me—you can bet your life that I ain't no fuckin' cocksucker. And you can take that to the fuckin' bank.

I like broads. Most people figure that out right away. People ask me, "Hey, Big Man, what are you? Are you an ass man, you like a can that can cancan? You a stem guy, you like legs that won't quit? What the fuck are you?"

I tell 'em, I'm a jug man. Jugs are for me. The bigger, the fuckin' better. Thirty-eight fuckin' double-D, ahhh-wooooo! Show me a pair of tits the size of basketballs and before long, I'm howlin' like fuckin' Pete the Nut. Ahhhh-wooooo.

Jugs. Jugs. Jugs! Biiiiig jugs. Any day of the fuckin' week.

*Show me a pair of tits the size of basketballs and before long, I'm howlin' like fuckin' Pete the Nut.*

Big juicy jugs! If you got a big pair of jugs, feel free to send the Big Man a photo: www.thekidfrombrooklyn.com. If you want to show 'em to me, I'll be more than happy to look at 'em.

## Michael Vick Is About as Smart as a Box of Rocks

You know that football quarterback, played for the Atlanta Falcons, who got sent to jail for fightin' dogs? Remember him? When that all went down, I must've gotten a fuckin' thousand e-mails: "What do you think of Michael Vick?"

I'll tell you what I think. I think he's a fuckin' asshole. I think he's a fuckin' jerk-off. I think he's dumber than a box of fuckin' rocks. I don't think he's got a brain in his fuckin' head. He threw away a hundred, two hundred million dollars in fuckin' endorsements.

*I always laugh when I hear college football players called student-athletes. Student, my ass.*

I always laugh when I hear college football players called student-athletes. Student, my ass. They got professors nowadays that let these guys skate. They play football for a college but it don't mean they're goin' to college.

You got guys comin' out of college football and into the pros these days that can't even fuckin' write their own name. Some guys go to college to learn. Some go to play football. Ain't no fuckin' in between.

## I Miss the Old Days When Dances Had Names

I remember back in the old days in Brooklyn, one of my favorite TV shows came on: Dick Clark's *American Bandstand*. Those were the days. He was always havin' the best guests on there: Frankie Avalon, Fabian, Connie Francis, Little Eva.

These celebrities would lip sync to their latest record and the dance floor would be filled with fresh-faced youngsters doing the latest dance. At least they had names for the dances back then. They had the Lindy Hop. The Twist. Remember the good ol' Stroll? Strooooooolin'. Oooh, yeah.

How about the Mashed Potatoes? Any of you readers remember how to do the fuckin' Mashed Potatoes? My favorite was Little Eva: "Everybody's doin' a brand-new dance now!" The fuckin' Locomotion!

Remember the Bird? Do the Bird! Do the Bird! Everybody fuckin' knows that the Bird's the word! Shimmy-shimmy koko bop! How about that? How about the old Cheek-to-Cheek? The dances had names back then.

What do they call the dances today? God only knows. The young people today don't even know who the fuck they're dancin' with. They dance ten fuckin' feet away from each other. And they look like they're havin' a fit, some kind of epileptic fit.

I expect those kids are gonna start foaming at the mouth any second. I want to jump in there and jam a tongue depressor in their fuckin' mouths just so they won't swallow their fuckin' tongues. And the dances ain't got no fuckin' name. Gimme some style. Don't give me that bullshit.

*Any of you readers remember how to do the fuckin' Mashed Potatoes?*

## Stop Putting Commercials on Cable TV

I don't know about the rest o' youse, but my cable bill is fuckin' out of control. Through the fuckin' roof. I'm payin' over two hundred dollars a fuckin' month. And despite the fact that I'm payin' an arm and a leg for somethin' that used to be free, I still got to watch all of those goddamn commercials.

And they gotcha by the nads. Every fuckin' station has got a fuckin' commercial every two minutes. You ever try to use the remote to avoid commercials? You can't fuckin' do it.

A commercial comes on, they're tryin' to sell me a fuckin' car, so I click to another station. Don't make no fuckin' difference. There's a commericial on that station, too. There, they're tryin' to sell me hamburgers. I go to a third station, it's got a commericial. They're tryin' to sell me beer. I go to a fourth station, it's got a commerical. They're showin' me fuckin' gross pictures tryin' to get me to fuckin' stop smokin', and I don't even fuckin' smoke!

Come on! It's a fuckin' conspiracy, that's what it is. They're

> *They're tryin' to get me to fuckin' stop smokin', and I don't even fuckin' smoke!*

tryin' to sell me chicken. They're tryin' to sell me fuckin' car insurance. They got it rigged. They put on the fuckin' commercials and we are gonna watch 'em!

I'm payin' through the fuckin' nose as it is. They charge me two hundred fuckin' dollars a month, they should have commercial-free cable television. They should have a station just for fuckin' commercials. That way, when I want to see a commercials, I can go to that station and see all the fuckin' commercials I want. And if I don't want to see any commercials, they should leave me the fuck alone.

## Nobody Gives a Fuck About a Midget

Do you know the group that has been discriminated against the most since the beginning of time? Midgets! That's right, midgets! Nobody gives a fuck about a midget and it ain't fuckin' fair.

You don't see any midgets in the military, do ya? I think a midget would make a helluva good soldier. But no. You don't see no midget cops, either. I know, I know what you're thinkin'. But believe me, growin' up in Brooklyn, I knew a lot of tough fuckin' midgets. They'd look up at a guy who was six foot six, grab him by his fuckin' balls, and squeeze him until he turned fuckin' green. They'd cut that giant down to size. They'd bring him to his fuckin' knees.

Still, I never seen no midget mailmen, no midget garbage

men, no midget construction workers, no midget airline pilots. Speakin' of the fuckin' airlines, they should let the midgets fly for free. Why not? They let all the kids fly for free. You could put two or three fuckin' midgets in one fuckin' seat and let 'em fly for free. Why the fuck not?

Come on! Give the fuckin' small people of the world a fuckin' break. Give fuckin' midgets a chance!

*Airlines should let the midgets fly for free. Why not? They let all the kids fly for free.*

## What's Your Favorite Name for a Fart?

In the English language, you can tell what's really important to people by the number of synonyms they got for it. I read somewhere that the word with the most synonyms in English is *drunk*. We think getting drunk is very important in this culture.

We also got a lot of synonyms for *fucking*: "getting laid," the "horizontal bop," "pourin' the pork," "meat injection," and so on. That's because poachin' a broad's eggs is very important to us.

We also got a lot of different names for *fart*. Back in Brooklyn when I was a kid, we called it "layin' a bomb." So I went on my Web site and I asked my viewers to get in touch and tell me their favorite name for a fart. Here's some of my favorites:

Egg Salad Smoothie
The One-Cheek Sneak

Pop Tarts
Prison Break
Talking Pants
Thunder in the Buns
Trouser Trombone
The Anal Salute
Blowing Kisses
Crap Duster
Heeeeeere Comes Johnny
Kill the Canary
Rectal Honk
Anal Evacuation
Ass Saxophone
Back Door Trumpet
Bean Bombers
Cheese Toastie
Blow Fish
Corn Hole Tremor
Frrrrrrapiccino
Brown Breeze
'Roid Scratcher
Butt Bugle
The Kelly Ripa, and last but not least . . .
The Sphincta Stinka

Holy fuck! Somebody light a fuckin' match! What's your favorite name for a fart? Let the Big Man know!

## There Ought to Be a Sign—Warning: Stutterer at the Drive-Through

The Big Man went to a White Castle the other night. That's right. White Castle. Even the Big Man likes a White Castle every now and again. I went to the one over there on Bergen Boulevard in Jersey and got in the drive-through line.

Took forever. I couldn't figure out why the line was moving so fuckin' slow. Finally I got up to the thing where you call in your order, and the guy went: "C-c-c-c-c-c-can I h-h-h-h-h-have, your order, p-p-p-p-p-p-lease?"

Now me, I ain't got nothin' against no fuckin' stutterers or anybody with a speech impediment. But, come on! Give me a fuckin' break. You can't have a guy at the drive-through line who fuckin' stutters.

"M-m-m-m-m-ay I h-h-h-h-help you, s-s-s-s-s-ir?"

I said, "Give me eight double cheeseburgers, a large fries, a large Diet Coke, and a large onion rings."

He then had to read back my order to make sure it was right. "Eight d-d-d-d-d-double ch-ch-cheeseburgers . . ."

I said, "Hey, pal, do me a favor and g-g-g-g-g-go f-f-f-f-f-fuck yourself! I'll come inside and order the fuckin' food."

## Even Goombahs Without Buttons Enjoy Dealing in Good Old-Fashioned Cash

Now, in my first book I told you the story of what every fuckin' Italian man in the world has to put up with. If you pay for something more expensive than a fuckin' six-pack of beer in cash, they think you must be with the Mafia. Well, truth is, about ninety-fuckin'-nine percent of us Italian men are not with the Mafia but we like to deal in cold, hard cash anyway. And here's my own personal reason why.

Credit cards suck donkey boners, that's why. Let me tell you about the last fuckin' time I used plastic. I have to mail some packages and buy some fuckin' stamps, so I go to the post office. The fuckin' post office. I'm standing in the fuckin' line, people gabbing their fucking mouths off on their fuckin' cell phones and me with a Duane Reade bag full of packages that need to go out. (Come to think of it, they weren't even my packages, they were Mona's packages, not that any of this shit is her fault.) Already I'm aggravated in two fucking ways. One, I got the long line that's moving slow; and, two, I got this old lady behind me who's griping about the slow line and making these fucking nauseating sounds with her fucking dentures. So finally, I get to the front of the line and I get a fuckin' Chinese teller who takes a fuckin' half hour putting postage on my packages.

She says, "Anything else?"

I says, "Yeah, I need a roll of fucking stamps."

"How will you pay?"

Here was my fucking mistake. I says, "With a fucking credit card, that's how the fuck I'm going to be paying."

She takes my card through that fucking little slot they got in the bulletproof glass on account of there's so much fucking crime these days. She swipes the fucker through a machine, makes a face like I just pissed down her leg, and swipes the card again. Now while she's doin' this, she's got a fuckin' three-way conversation goin' with the clerk on her right and the clerk on her left about post office benefits and how many fuckin' years you got to work before you can retire and some such shit, so she's only got about 5 fuckin' percent of her brain on what she's doin' with my fuckin' credit card.

"I cannot get it to go through," she says. "It says they will not accept your credit because of a 'court issue.'"

"What the fuck does that mean?" I says. "I ain't been fuckin' arrested and I ain't been served, so there ain't no fuckin' court issue."

"Sorry," she says. So I pay for my fuckin' packages and my roll of fuckin' stamps with cash. It comes to $71.23.

Now I need to figure out what the fuck this "court issue" is all about, so I go home, Mona brings me a grape soda, and I call my fuckin' credit card company. I get a machine. Press one to speak English, press two if you're from fuckin' Bangladesh, et-fuckin'-cetera.

I finally get a guy on the phone named Joachim, from the Frauds and Authorizations Department, and he says, "Mr. Caracciolo, there is no court issue that we know about, but there are two charges from the post office from about an hour ago, each for seventy-one dollars and twenty-three cents."

So I says, "Let me get this fuckin' straight. I paid for my packages and my stamps three times, twice by credit card and once in fuckin' cash?"

"Yes, sir. I want you to tell that clerk that I want to speak with her. She may be running a scam, charging your credit card and then pocketing your cash."

I thought about that for a minute and I said, "Nah. No way." She would have to be the greatest fucking criminal in the history of the fucking underworld to have a three-way conversation about how many fuckin years you got to work at the fuckin' post office before she could fuckin' retire, when English wasn't her fuckin' first language to begin with, and rip me the fuck off at the same time. She would have to be like fuckin' John Dillinger or Willie fuckin' Sutton to pull off a sweet scam like that. No, she just fucked up. I was pretty sure of that.

So I go back to the post office and I get the high-beam stares of hate from the poor mooks waiting in line as I cut to the front and go straight to the Chinese teller. I tell her the fuckin' credit card company said there was no court issue and that she fuckin' charged me twice for my shit, plus she took my fuckin' cash. She says that was impossible; the machine couldn't do that. I says it could, on account of it did. Well, it goes the fuck on and on, and by the time I get the two fuckin' charges taken off my credit card my whole fuckin' day is shot, and I never even get to finish my fuckin' grape soda before all the fuckin' bubbles are gone.

So now I'm a cash kind of guy, and it ain't got nothin' to do with no fuckin' Mafia.

## It Ain't Pretty at the All-You-Can-Eat Thanksgiving Buffet

I tell ya, there is nothing like greed and gluttony to ruin a man's appetite—and perhaps you have fuckin' figured out by now that I got an appetite that ain't easy to ruin. But it can happen. Here's a fucking example: one Thanksgiving a few years back, I decided to take Mona to a buffet. It was all you can fucking eat, $49.95.

The buffet was in a nice, classy hotel, in a fuckin' ballroom. So me and the missus sat down and then we went over to get some food. I took one plate. I got some turkey, a little stuffin', a little sweet potato, and a little cranberry sauce.

I went back to the table, ate the food on my plate, and stopped. I swear to my mother. I ate one plate and one plate only—and so did the missus. Why? I was watching everyone else eat and it put me off my food.

I mean, I never saw fuckin' people eat like that in my fuckin' life. They should have given these people fuckin' buckets and shovels to fill 'em up with. The gluttony was fucking nauseating, I want to tell ya!

There was one fuckin' woman there, she had two plates stacked fuckin' sky high with food. Gettin' back to the table, she was doing a fuckin' balancing act, making sure she didn't spill nothin. She had to duck so the top of her fuckin' mashed potatoes don't hit the fuckin' chandelier. She could've fed six fuckin' homeless men with all the food she had stacked on them fuckin' two plates.

And all the time she was screamin' at her fuckin' husband, who was still up at the buffet table: "Hey, Marty! Hey, Marty! Bring me back some more of that stuffin'. It's delicious!" This fuckin' woman ate like she was goin' to the fuckin' electric chair.

And I was lookin' at her. Where the fuck was she puttin' all of that fuckin' food? Then I looked all around me. Everybody was shovelin' it home. They were eatin' like there was no fuckin' tomorrow. It was a $49.95 all-you-can-eat buffet. They'd've felt fuckin' cheated—cheated!—if they just ate one fuckin' plate.

They should charge the rat bastards who go up there six, seven times the fuckin' price. They should eat their fuckin' hearts out.

*They should have given these people fuckin' buckets and shovels.*

## Merry Fuckin' Christmas

I wanna tell ya, the world is goin' wild. Goin' nuts. Out of fuckin' control. Take Christmas. It ain't just the postage stamps, which used to be great and now they fuckin' suck. They're tryin' to wipe Christmas out.

It was the most wonderful fuckin' time of the year, as Andy Williams used to sing. I took my seven-year-old niece to the

> *I want all of you readers, next time you go to a mall in December and there ain't no decorations, no tree, no Santa, I want youse to tell 'em to go fuck themselves.*

shopping mall in Jersey. Went inside, no Christmas decorations. No "Merry fuckin' Christmas" signs. No fuckin' Christmas tree.

I went into the big department store there and I got the manager.

I said, "Where's the Santa Claus? I want to take my niece to fuckin' see Santa."

He said, "No Santa Claus."

I said, "Go fuck yourself, you cocksucker. No decorations. No tree. No Santa. I'm goin' to some other fuckin' mall."

I want all of you readers, next time you go to a mall in December and there ain't no decorations, no tree, no Santa, I want youse to tell 'em to go fuck themselves. Then go to a fuckin' mall that has a Santa.

Christmas is a holiday for everybody. It's a fun holiday. Next year, when you do your fuckin' shopping, if they don't wish you a merry Christmas, you tell 'em to stick that merchandise right up their asses.

## When I'm in a Public Men's Room, I Don't Want Nothin' to Be Automatic

Sometimes the Big Man likes to cut loose on the weekend. Just get in the fuckin' car and drive. That's what I did a couple of months back. I got in the car and hit the Jersey turnpike. Free as a fuckin' bird. No aggravation!

But nature being what she is, soon enough I had to make a little pit stop, so I pulled over in one of them rest stops they got there on the turnpike. I went into the bathroom and took a leak. Then, since personal hygiene is important to me, I went to wash my hands. That's where my fuckin' problem started.

Where's the fuckin' spigots? The knobs? I wanted to turn the fuckin' water on. They got a faucet and that's it.

I said, "How the fuck do you get the water to come out?"

The guy next to me said, "There's no more handles. You got to put your hands under the faucet and the water comes out automatic."

Automatic, my fuckin' ass. I put my hands under there and the water came drippin' out. Drip . . . drip. What the fuck is that? I want to control my own flow of my fuckin' water. And I want the water to come out real fast.

*The guy next to me said, "There's no more handles. You got to put your hands under the faucet and the water comes out automatic."*

**Phil "Philly the Fuck-up" Nunziatta, the dumbest wiseguy in mob history. Tommy Funzi told him to collect $50K someone owed him and then kill the guy. Philly collected the money and chopped the guy up, then tossed the body parts into Dumpsters all around Brooklyn. He unfortunately mistook the guy's head for the $50K and dumped the money. He delivered the guy's head to Tommy Funzi instead. To no one's surprise, Philly ended up in a Dumpster himself. (photo courtesy U.S. Attorney's Office, Eastern District of New York)**

What's the story here? They got to have control of the fuckin' water now? What, is there a fuckin' water shortage? When you get done takin' a piss or a shit, you can't soap up real good and get your hands clean?

What, are you kiddin' me? With the prices they charge at them fuckin' rest stops, four dollars for a fuckin' dried-out hamburger, four dollars for a slice of pizza, two dollars for a fuckin' soda, they can't let you control your own water flow when you're washin' your fuckin' hands?

Give me a fuckin' break. Give me a faucet I can control myself. When I'm done takin' a hot piss or pinchin' off a massive loaf, I want to wash my hands fuckin' good.

## In Vegas, There Is Only One Color

Like I said, I been workin' in Vegas. Casa Di Amore. Doin'
my stand-up and observing life. One thing I noticed about
Las Vegas. No prejudice. They don't care if you're short, tall,
big, small. They don't care if you're black, white, Russian,
German, Jewish, Muslim. They don't give a flying fuck. Nobody gets treated any different from anyone else on account
of his skin color or his religion or anything like that. In Vegas,
there is only one fuckin' color.

Green.

I'm talkin' about the green in your pocket. As long as you
got that green in your pocket, that's all the fuck they care
about. That's the nature of Las Vegas, Nevada, and you can
take it straight from the Big Man.

You can shit and piss on the casino floor. They don't care.
You could jerk off and send your fuckin' baby batter flyin'
onto the roulette wheel and they'll say, "Excuse me, sir, let
me clean that up for you. Oh, there's still a little bit on your
dick, let me get that for you, too, sir."

As long as you got that green. And, of course, if you ain't got
that fuckin' green, you're in the bust-out hotel waitin' in the
buck ninety-nine buffet line with O.J. and reverend Fuckin' Al.

*You can shit and piss on the
casino floor. They don't care.*

# Either They're Makin' Popcorn or I'm in an Airport Security Line

You know the thing I can't stand the fuckin' most about travelin' today? When you go to the fuckin' airport and you're goin' through security, everybody's fuckin' got to take off his fuckin' shoes.

That's because they had that shoe-bomber asshole a few years back who tried to blow up a plane with some sparklers he had hidden in his shoe. They caught him trying to light a fuckin' wick attached to his fuckin' toe and saved the day, but now you can't get on a fuckin' plane without takin' off your fuckin' shoes. You got to take everything out of your pockets and put it on a conveyor belt and everyone's got to take his fuckin' shoes off.

Me? I got clean feet. I take two baths a day. But a lot of the fuckin' people you got flyin' with the fuckin' airlines these days, they ain't so conscientious about their fuckin' personal hygiene.

This is the one fuckin' time that I'm gonna agree with the fuckin' Muslim people. They should have foot baths right there on the security line, maybe just a little fuckin' dishwashing detergent in hot water—because some of these fuckin' people, *marone a mia*! Wash your fuckin' feet, people. For chrissakes! They fuckin' stink! I never smelled fuckin' feet like that in my fuckin' life.

If you like the fuckin' smell of stinky feet, this is like a dream fuckin' come true. All you got to do is go to the fuckin' airport and hang out in the security line all fuckin' day.

> *A lot of the fuckin' people you got flyin' with the fuckin' airlines these days, they ain't so conscientious about their fuckin' personal hygiene.*

## Mark My Words, They're Puttin' Somethin' in the Food

The Big Man goes to a lot of restaurants on account of he likes to eat. I been goin' to restaurants for years now and lately, I gotta tell you, I been seein' something I never saw before. It's a new fuckin' phenomenon. I can't go into an eating establishment these days without seeing fat kids. Fat kids!

Fat Asian kids! Holy fuck! You sure as fuck didn't have that back in my day. At first I thought there was a fuckin' Pop Warner Sumo league in my fuckin' neighborhood, but no.

There are fat Mexicans. I don't mean a little overweight or anything like that. I mean fat, like they were blown up like a fuckin' balloon. They're blown up like fuckin' Pillsbury Doughboys! Fuckin' enormous!

You can't fool me. The kids are the same. Their appetites are the same. It's the food that is fuckin' different. The fuckin' Food and Drug Administration ought to fuckin' look into this. What are they puttin' into the fuckin' food? They're puttin' some fuckin' additives into the food!

Growin' up in Brooklyn back when I was a kid, you ate Chinese food and an hour later you were fuckin' hungry again. Now you go into a restaurant and eat any type of fuckin' food, and you're hungry again an hour later.

Don't tell me there ain't no such thing as secret ingredients because I fuckin' know better. Years ago, Coca-Cola put real cocaine in their fuckin' soda pop.

So come on, FDA, let's figure out what the fuck is goin' on or else pretty soon we're gonna have to open up a new chain of fuckin' retail stores: Fat Kids Я Us.

Anyway, think about it! This is the Kid from Brooklyn, the Voice, the Voice of the People, signing off until next time, ladies and gentlemen. Visit my Web site at www.kidfrombrooklyn.com. And remember, the Big Man is always happy to see ya!